BST

FRIEND
OF ACPL

P9-CND-518

Protecting Your 401(k) and IRA

by Jennifer Lane, CFP, with Bill Lane

ALPHA

A member of Penguin Group (USA) Inc.

ALPHA BOOKS

Published by the Penguin Group

Penguin Group (USA) Inc., 375 Hudson Street, New York, New York 10014, USA

Penguin Group (Canada), 90 Eglinton Avenue East, Suite 700, Toronto, Ontario M4P 2Y3, Canada (a division of Pearson Penguin Canada Inc.)

Penguin Books Ltd., 80 Strand, London WC2R 0RL, England

Penguin Ireland, 25 St. Stephen's Green, Dublin 2, Ireland (a division of Penguin Books Ltd.)

Penguin Group (Australia), 250 Camberwell Road, Camberwell, Victoria 3124, Australia (a division of Pearson Australia Group Pty. Ltd.)

Penguin Books India Pvt. Ltd., 11 Community Centre, Panchsheel Park, New Delhi—110 017, India

Penguin Group (NZ), 67 Apollo Drive, Rosedale, North Shore, Auckland 1311, New Zealand (a division of Pearson New Zealand Ltd.)

Penguin Books (South Africa) (Pty.) Ltd., 24 Sturdee Avenue, Rosebank, Johannesburg 2196, South Africa

Penguin Books Ltd., Registered Offices: 80 Strand, London WC2R 0RL, England

Copyright © 2009 by Jennifer Lane

All rights reserved. No part of this book shall be reproduced, stored in a retrieval system, or transmitted by any means, electronic, mechanical, photocopying, recording, or otherwise, without written permission from the publisher. No patent liability is assumed with respect to the use of the information contained herein. Although every precaution has been taken in the preparation of this book, the publisher and authors assume no responsibility for errors or omissions. Neither is any liability assumed for damages resulting from the use of information contained herein. For information, address Alpha Books, 800 East 96th Street, Indianapolis, IN 46240.

THE COMPLETE IDIOT'S GUIDE TO and Design are registered trademarks of Penguin Group (USA) Inc.

International Standard Book Number: 978-1-59257-857-3
Library of Congress Catalog Card Number: 2008935070

11 10 09   8 7 6 5 4 3 2 1

Interpretation of the printing code: The rightmost number of the first series of numbers is the year of the book's printing; the rightmost number of the second series of numbers is the number of the book's printing. For example, a printing code of 09-1 shows that the first printing occurred in 2009.

Printed in the United States of America

Note: This publication contains the opinions and ideas of its authors. It is intended to provide helpful and informative material on the subject matter covered. It is sold with the understanding that the authors and publisher are not engaged in rendering professional services in the book. If the reader requires personal assistance or advice, a competent professional should be consulted.

The authors and publisher specifically disclaim any responsibility for any liability, loss, or risk, personal or otherwise, which is incurred as a consequence, directly or indirectly, of the use and application of any of the contents of this book.

Most Alpha books are available at special quantity discounts for bulk purchases for sales promotions, premiums, fund-raising, or educational use. Special books, or book excerpts, can also be created to fit specific needs.

For details, write: Special Markets, Alpha Books, 375 Hudson Street, New York, NY 10014.

Publisher: *Marie Butler-Knight*
Editorial Director: *Mike Sanders*
Senior Managing Editor: *Billy Fields*
Acquisitions Editor: *Michele Wells*
Development Editor: *Ginny Bess Munroe*
Production Editor: *Kayla Dugger*
Copy Editor: *Nancy Wagner*

Cartoonist: *Richard King*
Cover Designer: *Rebecca Harmon*
Book Designer: *Trina Wurst*
Indexer: *Heather McNeill*
Layout: *Brian Massey*
Proofreading: *John Etchison*

This book is dedicated to the idea that you can do anything you put your mind to.

Contents at a Glance

Contents

Introduction

When it comes to protecting your 401(k) and IRA, the power is in your hands. You have the power to ensure that it is large enough to provide security in retirement. While this might seem like a great deal of responsibility, it's actually a good idea. You can create the flexibility that you want. Your money can grow whether you continue to work steadily at a career or take some time off to go back to school or to raise kids; you can plan to retire early without waiting for a pension or Social Security to begin paying you.

Managing retirement and financial accounts can be a challenge, but not an insurmountable one if you understand the rules and do all the planning and careful management that employers used to do with workers' pensions. Whether you have a 401(k), an IRA, a 403(b), a SIMPLE IRA, or any of the varied retirement plans that you'll soon understand, each can be an important part of your retirement toolbox. Learning to manage these accounts can be fun—we show you how in this book.

Whether you're in your 20s and just starting your account, in your 30s or 40s and are building your nest egg, in your 50s—or even your 70s—and getting ready to retire, or you've been retired for years, we have the information you need to manage your accounts and protect your nest egg.

Extras

You'll find four types of sidebars in this book. These little snippets of information are geared toward keeping you out of trouble, providing tips, telling you what something means, or just giving you some inspiration and deeper context.

> **Rainy Days**
>
> Be sure to heed these warnings, which are meant to highlight the common retirement planning traps.

> **Nest Eggs**
>
> These insightful tips help you make the most of every planning opportunity.

> **Full Account**
>
> Sometimes, the best motivation to save for a secure retirement is the story of someone who's done it, either as an advisor or an investor. These messages will inspire you.

def•i•ni•tion _____

Finance and retirement planning is full of jargon and bureaucrat-ese. We give you clear meanings to the most arcane terminology.

Acknowledgments

It's pretty amazing how many people are involved in creating a book like this, which is less a collection of words on a page than a compilation of years of practice and experience. First we acknowledge the late William C. Lane, whose IRA provided the seed money that helped launch Jennifer's company. We're forever in his debt. And to Jennifer's clients, your willingness to share a very personal part of your lives with her continues to be a wonderful experience and has created many of the insights in this book.

Special thanks go to the team at Compass Planning Associates: John Perkins, CFP; Peggy Hughart; Sarah Heller; Heather Dmochowski; Catherine Heller; and Tom Vahey continue to be an enormous source of support and have kept the firm running beautifully while Jennifer has been writing this book. Although any remaining inadvertent errors remain ours alone, John and Peggy's willingness to also act as technical editors on the book has been very helpful.

And Jennifer owes a debt of gratitude to everyone at New England Cable News, past and present, both in the newsroom and in the booth. It's exciting to be able to interact with you and with viewers every week. The opportunity to work with you continues to be an invaluable one. And of course, to the viewers, if you keep e-mailing your questions, Jennifer will keep answering them.

Special Thanks to the Technical Reviewers

The Complete Idiot's Guide to Protecting Your 401(k) and IRA was reviewed by experts who double-checked the accuracy of what you'll learn here, to help us ensure that this book gives you everything you need to know about protecting your 401(k) and IRA. Special thanks are extended to Margaret Hughart and John Perkins.

Trademarks

All terms mentioned in this book that are known to be or are suspected of being trademarks or service marks have been appropriately capitalized. Alpha Books and Penguin Group (USA) Inc. cannot attest to the accuracy of this information. Use of a term in this book should not be regarded as affecting the validity of any trademark or service mark.

Part 1

Understanding Your Accounts

To begin, you learn about the task before you, the tools you have to work with, and the fundamentals of how to use them. We cover the basics of all the plans you might encounter, from the granddaddies—401(k) and IRA—right on through less-common 403(b) plans, 457 plans, and all the special plans, such as SIMPLE IRAs and SEP IRAs.

"These days, Danny, it's a 401(k) that's a girl's best friend."

Chapter 1

Retirement Accounts and Why You Need to Protect Them

In This Chapter

- ◆ New tax laws put you in the driver's seat
- ◆ Retirement saving is shifting from pensions to personal saving
- ◆ Special economic issues you need on your radar screen
- ◆ Making money management a priority
- ◆ The accounts you'll be managing

Improvements in health care, nutrition, and other factors mean people are living longer than ever. For example, baby boomers will live, on average, 20 years longer than their grandparents did. Of course this is great news, especially if you stay in good health, but a long retirement puts pressure on your nest egg to hold out as long as you do. If you plan to retire in your sixties or earlier, this could mean you'll live for 30 years or more in retirement—a long time to plan for. So it's never too early—or too late, for that matter—to start planning for a retirement that may be almost as long as your working career.

Becoming retirement ready and protecting your future security is up to you and is unrelated to how high or low your income is. We all live on limited resources; retirement security depends on focusing your resources on your goal. Before we formally introduce 401(k) plans and individual retirement accounts (IRAs), let's examine why they're more important now than ever.

You're in the Driver's Seat

New laws make it easier for Americans to save for their own retirement, but those same laws also make workers take more responsibility for their retirement savings success or failure. Among the most notable changes is a law that makes permanent new personal retirement accounts with large tax-saving incentives and an increase in the amounts that workers can deposit into their retirement accounts. Rules have been changed to make it easier to move accounts when a person changes jobs, and employers are now allowed to automatically enroll employees in company retirement plans and to redirect part of the employee's pay into the account unless the employee opts out of the plan.

Nest Eggs

To encourage saving, retirement plans have a variety of tax benefits that save you money. Investment earnings and interest in retirement accounts aren't taxed until they're withdrawn, and deposits into many types of retirement accounts are tax-deductible. Throughout this book, you learn to take advantage of these tax savings to help build your retirement security.

The government is encouraging people to save for retirement with these new laws. Regardless of how you feel about the policy itself, it's important to take the government's hint and take ownership of your retirement security.

Government employers and some large corporations still have *defined-benefit pension plans* that guarantee workers income in retirement based on their tenure with the company and how much they were paid. Most other employers, even some who may have offered a pension benefit in the past, now have retirement plans that workers are responsible for managing themselves. These employee-managed accounts are called *defined-contribution plans*. Income in retirement from a defined-contribution plan depends on the amount you contributed to the plan while you were working and how much your investments grew.

def•i•ni•tion

> **Defined-benefit pension plans** (pensions, by a more familiar name) are plans that pay a specific retirement benefit once certain requirements, like years of service or age, are met. **Defined-contribution plans** have specific rules that dictate when deposits can be made, who can make them, and how much the deposit can be.

Policymakers have created a variety of defined-contribution plans to encourage workers to save for retirement because they know they're going to need the money. The economic and social trends warn that government aid might not fill the full bill for most retirees. They want to encourage the workers to save part of their pay while they're working so they can spend it later in retirement.

Reading the Warning Signs

You are the person responsible for your retirement, so keep an eye on these important trends: Social Security benefits, tax rates, inflation, and health-care costs.

Social Security

If you're working in a nongovernment job, Social Security taxes are withheld from your paycheck. Most government employees pay into a separate government pension instead of Social Security. If you're self-employed, Social Security taxes are part of your self-employment tax payment.

> **Nest Eggs**
>
> By 2008 rules, up to 85 percent of a person's Social Security retirement income benefit may be taxable. Workers pay Social Security tax on their first $102,000 of earnings.

The amount of Social Security retirement benefits you'll ultimately collect is based on how much you pay into the system while you're working. But you can't think of Social Security as a savings account; the program doesn't put your money away until it's time for you to draw it out. Social Security is a pay-as-you-go system, meaning payments you make now are quickly turned into this month's payment to current retirees. This system works fine as long as many workers are paying taxes and not too many retirees are receiving benefits.

Rainy Days

Social Security income payments increase each year based on a version of the Consumer Price Index called the CPI-W, which tracks price increases on the kinds of goods and services bought by active workers. As a retiree, your cost of living may be greater than current workers' if expenses like health care grow faster than the CPI-W.

Unfortunately for the Social Security system's health, the number of retirees is increasing rapidly compared to the number of workers. We can expect the Social Security Administration to compensate for this shift by altering future benefits. These changes might include increasing the age when an individual can begin drawing full retirement benefits, making a larger percentage of income benefits taxable, or making less-generous inflation increases to benefits each year. Regardless of how the government adjusts your benefit, the result is sure to be that you'll rely more on your own savings for retirement security and less on your Social Security income.

Taxes

Many people assume their income taxes will be lower when they retire because they won't be earning taxable wages. Unfortunately, this isn't always the case. More of an individual's income may be taxable after he retires than he might expect. Part of everyone's Social Security income is taxable, and withdrawals from most retirement plans are taxable as income, too. If you have a pension, some or all of its benefits might be taxable. What's more, income tax rates could increase by the time you retire. Higher tax rates aren't out of the question as the government struggles to close recent budget deficits and pay a massive federal debt. Income taxes could continue to be one of your biggest expenses even after you retire. So regardless of the reasons, it's important to consider the effect of this cost when managing your retirement accounts and planning your savings goals.

Rainy Days

> If you work for the government and expect a pension but also worked for a private employer and paid Social Security taxes, there's no guarantee you'll collect 100 percent of both benefits. Check the Social Security website, www.ssa.gov, for a worksheet to calculate what you should receive under the so-called windfall provision.

Inflation

Planning for price increases on the things you buy—inflation—is an important part of protecting your retirement nest egg. Inflation causes nest egg damage when higher prices force you to make bigger withdrawals from your retirement accounts than you'd planned.

Nest Eggs

> Many people are happy to give you advice, but you're the one who's most invested in the health of your retirement accounts. Hire help and pay for advice when you need it, but don't forget that understanding your accounts and managing your investments is ultimately up to you. Stay involved. Your advisors should be partners, not sole managers of your accounts.

The government regularly measures inflation and gives reports on what's called the Consumer Price Index or CPI. Paying attention to changes in the CPI is one way of gauging how your living expenses might be changing. Social Security benefits are adjusted every year for CPI inflation. However, many of your expenses in retirement might increase at a rate faster than the CPI. Increasing costs of home mainte-nance and medical care are two expenses where inflation can do heavy damage to your nest egg if you haven't planned on making larger and larger yearly withdrawals from your accounts to compensate.

Health Care

Unforeseen medical expenses and high health insurance premiums can be a huge drain on your retirement assets, especially if you're not in tip-top health. Some aspects of your health-care costs are within your control. Maintaining a good weight, eating good food and limiting junk food, exercising regularly, quitting smoking, and seeing your doctor regularly are all ways you can reduce your risk of high medical costs in retirement by staying healthy now. As the baby boom generation ages and puts a strain on the nation's health-care system, health insurance premiums and the cost of health care are likely to increase. Protect your retirement nest egg by allowing for these costs in your retirement budget.

Living Longer Requires a Bigger Nest Egg

Lengthening life spans, improved health care, and a growing emphasis on the well-being of massive numbers of aging baby boomers means your post-career years should be long and active. Even if you decide to adopt a part-time retirement job, your nest egg at retirement must be large enough to live as long as you do. The importance of building a healthy nest egg has never been greater.

Full Account

Don't let the complexity of retirement plan rules—or anything about your finances—intimidate you. You're not stupid. It may not be easy, and it's not always fun, but you're up to the challenge, and the rewards are worth the investment of time and energy. If it were easy and fun, we'd all be talking about it every chance we got; the benefits of this new obscure tax law or that new investment strategy would be the hot topic of conversation at every weekend cookout. Let's face it: we need to understand how to protect our retirement plans because we live in a new world. Your financial security is now more on your shoulders than at any time since before President Roosevelt's New Deal, so don't be afraid or reluctant to ask a professional for help. I've worked with all sorts of brilliant clients over the years—engineers, teachers, researchers, executives, scientists, and even other financial planners. They weren't shy about asking for advice, and you shouldn't be either. If nothing else, you'll learn important financial lessons and become financially secure more quickly.

M&Ms: Staying on Track

Life is hectic, and there never seems to be enough time to get through those ever-growing to-do lists. It's easy to lose sight of the big picture and let some of the financial planning, such as investing and creating retirement accounts, take a backseat to paying monthly credit card bills and daily expenses. But don't do it! Make retirement planning much easier by making it a regular part of your monthly money meetings.

Monthly money meetings (we call them M&Ms) are an important part of keeping your finances on track. Plan a monthly financial review with your spouse or partner, and involve your children in the meetings as well. Children need to feel financially connected as young as possible and gain a sense of sharing the financial responsibilities with their parents. If you're single, you're not off the hook. Regular M&Ms are important for everyone because they keep your finances top-of-mind and your goals on track.

M&M Checklist

In your money meetings, review and update your financial and retirement goals. Some things you can check and discuss each month, and others you should review periodically throughout the year.

In each monthly meeting:

♦ List your income and expenses.

♦ Discuss upcoming expenses and long-term spending goals.

♦ Decide whether the cash allowances you're taking are enough to cover entertainment expenses and extras.

With most couples, one person pays the bills, and the other person is less involved in the family finances. Monthly money meetings keep both in the loop and give each person a chance to discuss finances in an unstrained, structured atmosphere.

Each monthly meeting is part of a financial season—or fiscal quarter, if you'd rather think of it that way.

By following M&M seasons, you'll be sure to review all the parts of your financial plan each year. Here is how you can break out the seasons:

Winter: First quarter of the year

♦ Tax planning, part I—Gather your tax information for your tax return.

♦ Budget planning—Check the expenses from last year and make sure you're not spending more than you're earning, receiving from pension or Social Security, or that you can afford to take from your nest egg.

♦ If you're retired and have Social Security or pension income, review the payments you expect to receive this year and decide how much you should be taking from your retirement nest egg each month as income (see Chapter 12).

♦ Investment planning—Check year-end reports and decide if you need to change any investments. Check the asset allocation of your portfolio and rebalance if you need to.

Spring: Second quarter of the year

♦ Tax planning, part II—Decide whether you need to make any changes to your withholding, estimated tax payments, or investments based on the results of your tax return.

♦ Credit, debt, and ID theft protection—Check your credit report from one agency. If you're working on paying down debt, decide whether you want to continue on the same payment schedule or add more to the principal to retire the debt faster.

♦ Insurance—Review your insurance policies and make changes as needed.

Summer: Third quarter of the year

♦ Estate planning—Check your estate plan and beneficiaries to see if you need to change anything.

♦ Credit, debt, and ID theft protection—Check your credit report from another of the three credit reporting agencies. Change the passwords on your online accounts.

◆ Financial planning—Review your financial goals and update your retirement and financial plan. Read a financial planning book or one on investing.

Fall: Fourth quarter of the year

◆ Tax planning, part III—Check your year-to-date income and see if there are any year-end tax-planning tasks you should consider. Check-in with your tax accountant for help.

◆ Investment planning—Check your investments, and decide whether to rebalance and harvest any capital gains.

◆ Charitable giving—Plan charitable giving for the year.

Nest Eggs

There are three credit-reporting bureaus, and each owes you a free report once every 12 months. Go to www.AnnualCreditReport.com. Remember the report is free; the site may try to sell you your credit score and credit monitoring, but all you need is the free report.

Feeling Secure

Protect your retirement accounts from one of their biggest enemies: you! Avoid living on your entire paycheck. Let the magic of long-term investing and *compound interest* work for you by always saving part of your pay. Saving some of your earnings toward emergency cash and part of them toward retirement will not only ensure that you'll feel financially secure from month to month but will also help keep your lifestyle from outpacing your ability to afford it in retirement.

def•i•ni•tion

Compound interest is interest that is paid not only on the principal you have saved but also on the accumulated interest from prior periods that you have not withdrawn.

Your retirement income will probably include Social Security and/or pension income; income from investments; and withdrawals from your savings and retirement plans. Many people, and an increasing number at that, also choose to work at least part-time in retirement, adding earned income to the mix as well. Part of protecting your retirement accounts will be to create this multi-part stream of income sources. It will be easier to manage your taxes in retirement if you have the added security of investments and savings outside of your retirement plans as well as pension or Social Security income and part-time work.

Many people make the mistake of not contributing to their retirement plans or contributing too little because they expect an inheritance from family to fund their retirement nest egg. Inheritances are sufficient retirement nest eggs for only a very few. Many people who expect inheritances are stunned to learn their relatives spent all or most of their supposed bequest on their own expenses, such as medical care, or that the inheritance was much smaller than hoped, if it ever existed at all. Relatives are often uncomfortable talking about money. Don't count on an inheritance funding your retirement unless you have had enough discussions with your family members and their financial advisors to be absolutely sure. Retirement is not something you can guess at and then redo when your assumptions turn out wrong.

What's more, people often underestimate the amount of money needed to retire. A parent may honestly believe he is leaving a plentiful inheritance to his children and may tell them so. Without knowing the specifics, it would be foolish for heirs to bank on it.

Retirement Planning Rules of Thumb

You can plan for a secure retirement only if you have an idea of what you're shooting for. In future chapters, we help you refine your retirement savings goals and set the size of your target nest egg, but here are some good rules of thumb.

Save at least 10 to 15 percent of your income toward retirement. Saving this amount will help build your nest egg and keep you living a lifestyle that accommodates your habitual savings. The savings cushion you create in your budget will give you some flexibility if temporary expenses—like child care costs, job loss, or major medical costs—force you to stop saving for a while. It will also ensure that the lifestyle you get used to while you're working isn't so expensive that you have difficulty saving enough to cover it later.

Your retirement income should come from a diversified selection of sources: Social Security or pension payments, retirement plan withdrawals, and investment earnings. As a rough estimate, save and invest enough so you won't need to withdraw more than 3 or 4 percent per year from your retirement plans and investments to supplement Social Security or pension to meet your retirement income needs. Following that rule of thumb, if your retirement nest egg totals $500,000 and you're retiring today, plan on withdrawing no more than $20,000 of your nest egg each year.

Over the course of your work life, any number of circumstances could interrupt—or at least reduce—your ability to save for retirement. The key is to not let these interruptions derail you permanently. If you're diligent about regularly saving, short-term setbacks won't derail you as long as you keep your eye on your goal of protecting your nest egg and achieving your retirement goal.

> **Nest Eggs**
>
> Don't decide not to save for retirement because you think it's hopeless and there's no way you can possibly save 10 percent of your income! Instead, start today with just 1 percent. Add a percentage point each time you get a raise or a cash windfall. Once saving is on your radar screen, you'll be amazed at the places you find money to invest.

Introducing 401(k)s and IRAs

Social Security and even pension income is rarely enough to cover all your expenses in retirement, especially as time goes on and inflation increases the cost of living. You need a retirement nest egg that you control and can use to offset the affects of inflation on your retirement income. This should include investments in retirement accounts that bestow tax advantages, such as an *individual retirement account* (*IRA*) or an account provided through your job, most commonly a *401(k)*.

def•i•ni•tion

> **Individual retirement accounts (IRAs)** are retirement plan accounts that carry a tax advantage intended to encourage savings. **401(k)** plans are employer-sponsored retirement savings incentive programs that take their name from the snippet of the Internal Revenue Code that created them in 1978.

Accounts You'll See at Work: 401(k)s

Never has a dull patch of bureaucrat-speak become so famous that millions of ordinary Americans refer to it by name in water-cooler chats at work, in financial planning discussions with advisors, or at the kitchen table. 401(k) plans grew rapidly in popularity starting in the mid-1980s when companies and employees alike discovered that retirement plans that made contributions directly from employee paychecks could become a core employee benefit.

Companies liked them because they were less expensive than traditional defined-benefit pension plans, which required larger employer contributions and cost employers more. Employees liked 401(k)s, which are a kind of defined-contribution plan, because they were more portable than pensions. In a workforce that is increasingly mobile and less likely to work for a single company for an entire career, one of the most popular features of 401(k)s is that they're easily moved from one employer to the next or even into an account that the employee manages, something that's not always possible with a pension plan.

Many employers give their retirement plan a descriptive name like employee savings plan or savings plan, but most simply call their plans 401(k)s. If you work for a large for-profit company, your plan likely goes by that name. If your employer is a nonprofit, a school, or a hospital, your plan is probably called a 403(b). Other special plans are named after their own parts of the tax code called 457 plans and 401(a) plans. If you work for a small company or if you're self-employed, you might have a *SIMPLE* plan or a *SEP IRA* plan. We cover how to harness the financial power of all these plans in the next few chapters.

def•i•ni•tion

SIMPLE plans are special IRA accounts set up through your employer. You make contributions to your SIMPLE IRA through payroll deduction, and your employer matches it—usually 100 percent of what you contribute, up to 3 percent of your pay.

SEP IRAs are IRA accounts meant for self-employed individuals, but some small businesses use them as well. You don't need to be self-employed full-time to have a SEP IRA. Subject to an inflation-adjusted cap, you can contribute up to 20 percent of any self-employment income (after business expenses). Or, if you work for a small business that withholds payroll taxes for you, your employer can contribute up to an extra 25 percent of your pay to your SEP account.

While the federal government gave life to these plans, we emphasize that managing these plans—selecting investments from a list of choices and deciding how much to invest in the plan—is entirely up to you. These are your accounts, and aside from a few exceptions, even your retirement plan at work is separate from your employer's assets. This means that if your employer goes out of business, your retirement plan account is not in jeopardy—it's not an asset your employer's creditors can look at to pay off company debts. This provides protection and peace of mind in a tough economy, but at the same time, the government is sending a strong signal through the legislation it's enacting: a comfortable retirement is, more than ever, your responsibility.

Similar to the rules of the road you had to study when getting your drivers license, the Employee Retirement Income Security Act (*ERISA*) sets the minimum standards that the employer has to follow in managing your retirement benefit plans. The employer must have a plan document that describes:

def•i•ni•tion

> **ERISA** is the Employee Retirement Income Security Act. Created in 1974, ERISA is the federal law that sets the standards for employee retirement and health-care benefits.

- ◆ The day-to-day operation and benefits of the plan
- ◆ A separate trust fund to hold the employees' accounts
- ◆ A record-keeping system
- ◆ Documents to keep you up to date on your account balance and activity like deposits and earnings.

The separate trust fund requirement is what keeps your retirement money safe from the fortunes of the company.

Accounts You Can Open Yourself

Whether or not your employer offers a retirement plan, if you or your spouse has earnings from work, you can invest in personal retirement accounts that you open yourself: an IRA or a Roth IRA. Like the plans at work, these personal accounts have rules that limit the amount you can contribute each year. These accounts are separate from your job, so you can't invest in them directly through your paycheck, but depending on your income and whether you have a retirement plan at work, you might be able to deduct the amount you deposit in an IRA on your tax return. This deduction saves you income taxes just as if you had contributed to your employer's plan through your paycheck.

One advantage these personal retirement accounts have is that you can pick almost any investment you'd like for your account. You're not limited by the list your employer has chosen for your company's 401(k) plan. The choices available in an IRA may seem overwhelming at first, but once you've learned how to pick your investments, this extra control you have makes your personal retirement accounts a powerful way to grow your retirement nest egg.

While there's probably a small risk that your mutual fund provider or *certificate of deposit* (*CD*) issuer will go insolvent, it's prudent to understand how your investment accounts are insured. The IRA accounts you open yourself will contain investments that should have either Federal Deposit Insurance Corp. (FDIC) or Securities Investor Protection Corp. (SIPC) insurance coverage. FDIC insurance protects your cash deposits up to $100,000 from loss in the unlikely event your bank fails. Look for FDIC insurance on your CDs and your *money market deposit account* at your bank or credit union. FDIC insurance is limited to $100,000 per person at each individual bank. That means that if you have a savings, a checking, and a CD at one bank and all the accounts are in your name alone, you have full coverage if the total of all the accounts is less than $100,000.

def•i•ni•tion

A **certificate of deposit (CD)** is a bank's promissory note to repay the amount deposited, with interest, at a future date, typically one month to five years. A **money market deposit account** often pays lower interest than a CD, but the money is accessible anytime without waiting for a future maturity date.

Not all money market accounts carry FDIC insurance. Accounts without this coverage may only be as safe as the company that issues them. Read the information provided about the money market—the prospectus—carefully before you invest to be sure your money is safe.

SIPC insurance is funded by premiums paid by broker-dealers, like Fidelity Investments, Charles Schwab, and Vanguard Investments. SIPC insurance covers losses of assets from brokerage accounts, the deposits that brokers use to finance stock, bond, and other securities transactions.

The Least You Need to Know

- ◆ Monthly money meetings are essential for ensuring that your entire family understands and is working toward a common goal.

- ◆ One of the most important safeguards against the unexpected is regularly saving at least 10 percent of your pay for emergency expenses and retirement savings.

- ◆ Because you're likely to live as much as 30 years or more in retirement, caring for your health starting today will safeguard your nest egg against high health-care bills.

- ◆ Tax-advantaged accounts such as 401(k)s and IRAs can be powerful tools for helping your retirement income keep up with inflation.

Chapter 2

How They Work: 401(k)

In This Chapter

◆ Why 401(k) accounts are so important to your retirement

◆ Picking your investment

◆ Changing jobs

◆ Getting money out of your 401(k) before retirement

"Your retirement security is up to you." That's the clear message behind the movement away from employer-managed and -funded pension plans to employee-managed and -funded (with a bit of incentive payment from your employer) 401(k) plans. As ominous as it may sound, this trend toward individual responsibility for retirement financial security is not all bad. Defined-contribution plans, as 401(k) and similar plans whose success relies on individual contributions are called, are more portable and less expensive than traditional pension plans. This works in your favor when you change jobs, and it helps lower costs for the employer, which should, in theory at least, help the company's bottom line and keep you employed.

With control comes responsibility, and growing your 401(k) is *your* responsibility. The money you'll have to spend in retirement depends on the amount you save from your paycheck and the success you have in your investment choices. In this chapter, we help you understand the basics of how your 401(k) plan works and how to select among the investment choices your plan gives you.

The Basics: Contributing to Your 401(k)

As we explained in Chapter 1, a 401(k) is a tax-deferred account similar to an IRA (see Chapter 3), with a couple of important exceptions: you contribute to your 401(k) directly from your paycheck, and the money you contribute is pretax regardless of your income. These features make 401(k)s a little easier to manage than IRAs.

Employer Setup

Your employer has gone through the trouble to set up the account and has selected a variety of investments for you to pick from. Your contributions are easily made from your paycheck, and you don't need to keep track of eligibility rules and caps on deposits; your employer does that for you.

But you can contribute to the 401(k) only while working for your current employer. If you don't have an account at your current job, but you do from a previous job, you can't contribute to the old plan unless you convert that account to an IRA. We give more detail on changing jobs and managing old 401(k) accounts in Chapter 8.

Nest Eggs

Contributions to 401(k) plans save money because you don't pay income taxes on the amount you contribute until you make a withdrawal. Social Security, Medicare, and federal unemployment taxes are still applied to your whole paycheck—including the amount automatically deposited into the 401(k) plan—so making smart contributions to your retirement account won't reduce your government benefits.

Higher Contributions

You can contribute more to a 401(k) than you can to an IRA. In 2008, you could contribute up to $15,500 or 100 percent of your pay, whichever is lower, to your plan. If you are age 50 or older, you could add a catch-up amount of $5,000, for a total of $20,500. Both of these limits increase with inflation starting in 2009.

Employers Can Pitch In

As part of an overall benefits plan, your employer might also contribute to your 401(k) account. This amount is in addition to your salary and gets the same tax treatment as your contributions do. Contributions are not taxable to you when deposited into the account but are taxed as income when withdrawn.

Companies can choose how much they want to put into employees' accounts, with a few restrictions to be sure all employees are treated fairly. Contributions are made as profit sharing or matching contributions that depend on how much an individual is contributing. Under profit sharing, which interestingly has nothing to do with whether your company is profitable, the employer can decide each year whether to contribute to the employees' plans.

Matching contributions mean that the employer promises to match a certain percentage of each employee's contribution up to a specific percentage of her pay. Many employers match all of the first 3 percent that a person contributes, and others match 50 percent of the first 6 percent that one contributes. The matching feature is the employer's way of encouraging workers to contribute to their 401(k) accounts. The first matching example encourages employees to put at least 3 percent into their plan. The second puts the bar a little higher—at 6 percent—but the result in both cases is a maximum match from the employer of 3 percent of the employee's salary.

More and more employers are establishing *safe-harbor 401(k)* plans to save themselves the effort and cost of running the non-discrimination tests each year.

def•i•ni•tion

More and more employers are establishing **safe-harbor 401(k)** plans to save them the effort and cost of running the nondiscrimination tests each year. Among other characteristics, safe-harbor plans make employer contributions 100 percent vested immediately, just like your personal contributions.

Safe-harbor plans make employer contributions 100 percent vested immediately, just like your personal contributions.

Full Account

I think it would surprise many to know that the amount of money people have invested in their retirement accounts is not always related to their incomes. I've met with clients who've always earned a modest salary, but who have plenty in their retirement nest egg and who max out their 401(k) accounts each year. And I have clients with high incomes who struggle to save.

In the end, it's really not about how much you make that makes the biggest difference in the robustness of your retirement accounts; it's your priorities. If you decide you want to spend all your income now, that's up to you. Most people eventually reach a point in their lives when they can see further down the horizon, and long-term financial security becomes more important than short-term spending. That's when they're ready to focus on their 401(k)s and start growing their security. If you're not there yet, bite the bullet, and at least contribute enough to your 401(k) to qualify for an employer match. And once you start, you might find that seeing your account grow is addictive!

Participation at All Levels

Not everyone can afford to contribute to a 401(k). The IRS might allow you to put $15,500 into your account, but that doesn't mean you can afford to! What often happens is that the higher-paid people in the company want to put the maximum they can into the 401(k), and the lower-paid people put less than the maximum. ERISA rules require that the plan be fair for everyone and define certain tests the plan must pass to prove it's treating everyone fairly. The matching formulas and profit-sharing contributions that companies use are related to meeting these tests.

Vesting

Your own contributions to your 401(k) plan are always 100 percent vested. This means that when you leave your job, you can take the amount you have put into the account with you—it's not forfeited to your employer. The contributions your employer makes may not be as portable, though. A vesting schedule dictates when the contributions your employer makes to your account really become yours.

There are two types of vesting schedules: cliff and graded. Cliff vesting is an all-or-nothing proposition. Not a penny of your employer's contribution is yours until you reach a specified work anniversary, and then every dime is yours. Because 401(k) plans and employer contributions are an important part of attracting new employees, most employers who use cliff vesting allow employees to vest at three years or they use a graded vesting schedule. Under graded vesting, employer contributions vest in stages or grades. In many cases you may be partly vested as early as your second anniversary. The first grade is usually 20 percent, and then your vesting percentage increases each year until you are fully vested after completing five years of service.

Nest Eggs

Vesting is based on years of service, not just the years you participate in the 401(k). If you've been in a job for a couple of years without contributing to a 401(k), it's not too late to take advantage of employer matching. Even if you leave in another year or two, you may be more vested than you think because of your total years of service.

Rule Book

The book of rules that govern your specific 401(k) plan is called the Summary Plan Description (SPD). Your human resources department will give you a copy of the Summary Plan Description when you start work, or it might be available on the company website.

The SPD outlines when you'll be eligible to participate and the specifics about how to contribute to the account and how to withdraw money. Most companies allow employees over age 21 to start participating in their 401(k) fairly quickly—usually within 30 to 90 days of joining the company—but the employer match might not start until you've been with the company longer. Don't let the delayed match feature discourage you from starting your contributions. Remember, your retirement security is up to you, and a 401(k) plan is a great tool to have in your retirement toolbox.

Beneficiaries

You need to list a beneficiary on your 401(k) account and keep the designation up-to-date. Like your IRA and other retirement plans, your 401(k) assets can pass to your beneficiaries directly without waiting for the probate process and your will. Also, the beneficiary can choose to continue the tax-deferral you started by leaving the money in the 401(k) or transferring it to an IRA (see Chapter 13). So be sure to list a beneficiary on your 401(k) account and update it as needed.

Your 401(k) Investment Choices

Employers are required to pick a list of investment offerings for the 401(k) plan as part of choosing the company they hire to administer your plan. These plan providers are often familiar, big-name investment brokers like Fidelity Investments and Vanguard Group. Insurance companies like Principal Financial Group Inc. and Prudential Financial Inc. provide 401(k) plans, as well. The plan provider acts as the plan trustee and handles all the complicated back-office operations required of a 401(k) plan.

Plan providers send you regular account statements and provide access to your account online. They coordinate with the plan administrator who's responsible for managing the tax and legal aspects of the plan. If you have questions about your plan that you can't answer yourself by reading the Summary Plan Document, your employer might refer you to the plan administrator for an answer.

Don't let fluctuations in your account balance discourage you from continuing to make contributions from each paycheck. Investing the same amount on a regular schedule as the market goes up and down in value is known as *dollar cost averaging*. This can help reduce the investment risk in your account over time.

def•i•ni•tion

Investing the same dollar amount at fixed intervals, such as each payday, is called **dollar cost averaging**. Because share prices increase and decrease daily, a regular investment buys fewer shares when prices are up and more shares when prices are down. Over time, this strategy can boost your investment performance.

The money in your 401(k) is invested according to the choices you make from among the menu of investment options. If you don't choose one, the plan will invest your money in the default fund. Until recently, most plans had the stable value or money market fund as the default. Employers chose this account to protect the account from losing value, but for many employees this account was too conservative to be a good choice as a retirement investment. After recent ERISA rule changes, employers now use a *target-date fund* as the default fund. In the end, this fund may be the best choice for you, but research the choices and check for yourself.

def•i•ni•tion

> **Target-date funds** are mutual funds whose allocations of stocks, bonds, and cash change as the portfolio moves closer to a time-specific event, such as retirement.

Simplified Investing

The plan provider and your employer want to make it easy for you to understand the investments in your plan. The plan's website will contain a questionnaire to help you decide how much risk you are comfortable taking with your investments. There will also be a list of the investment choices. Most plans use Internet links in their online investment lists that link to information about each fund. If you don't already know your optimal mix of investments—your asset allocation—start a new plan by completing the risk questionnaire your plan offers and check the recommended investment mix. Then check the list of choices for the strongest funds in each asset allocation category.

Don't just pick the funds that have performed the best recently. Ideally, the funds you pick should have these characteristics:

- Be rated a 4- or 5-star fund by Morningstar (www.Morningstar.com).

- Have performed at least as well as their *benchmark* over the past one, three, and five years.

- Have an *annual expense ratio* of 1.5 percent or lower.

def•i•ni•tion

A **benchmark** is a standard used to compare performance, such as benchmarking a fund that invests in large company stocks against the Standard and Poor's 500 Index. The **annual expense ratio** is the percentage of the plan's assets that are paid to cover operating, management, and marketing costs.

Chapter 7 explains how to pick investments and decide on an asset allocation, but for now, if your plan offers a target-date fund, consider starting your contributions by investing in the target-date fund that matches your expected retirement year.

Fees

Your 401(k) plan has two sets of fees: administrative and investment. Both are paid by the plan—you won't get a bill—but because fees are paid from plan funds, they affect the performance of your account. Administrative fees cover the cost of running the plan itself. This includes expenses such as the cost of preparing annual reports, running required discrimination tests, and supporting the website and customer service department you use to interact with your plan.

Investment fees exist within the investing account in the plan. You won't see the administrative costs of the plan, but you can check on the investment costs. Some larger companies, which have 401(k) plans with high balances and a lot of employee participants, negotiate with the 401(k) provider to reduce the investment fees in the plan. You can check the regular fees on your 401(k) funds using the fund prospectus, www. Morningstar.com, or the fund's website. Then check with your employer to see if your plan has waived the regular sales fees.

Nest Eggs

Most plans let you change your investment choices anytime, but some plans limit changes to a couple times a year. Rebalancing once a year—automatically if your plan offers this service— is the best way to keep your plan on track (see Chapter 7).

Rainy Days _____

> Many 401(k) plans offer primarily mutual funds as their investment choices. Mutual funds have lower fees than the other common 401(k) investment—annuities. If your 401(k) uses annuities with expense ratios higher than 1.5 percent, you need to decide whether investing in a less expensive IRA is a better alternative for you.

401(k) Investing While You're Still Working

Plan your budget so you are building your emergency savings account as well as adding to the 401(k). A good rule of thumb is to direct 10 percent of your pay to savings until you've accumulated three to six months' worth of your basic living expenses. At the same time, try to contribute at least enough to the 401(k) plan to qualify for any employer match. Once you've filled your savings account, reduce the savings to 1 or 2 percent of your pay, and divert what you were previously saving to the 401(k). If 10 percent seems unreachable on your budget, in Chapter 6 we offer some ideas on making your budget work better.

Your 401(k) account can go with you when you change jobs. You can't move your 401(k) account while you're still at the sponsoring employer, but once you're gone, you can move your account to your new employer's plan or to your own IRA. If you love your old employer's 401(k) plan for its investment choices or its low cost, you may find you can leave the money where it is. Most employers will let you keep your money in their 401(k) plan even if you're not working for them anymore. You can't contribute to the plan, but you can work with the investments and manage the account.

If you choose to move your money, you can do it by using either a 60-day rollover or a direct transfer. The direct transfer—or trustee-to-trustee transfer—is by far the better of the two choices because the money is transferred either electronically or by paper check directly between your old plan provider and your new one and is never placed in your name. You don't take control of the money, so you won't run the risk of not completing the transfer into the new plan.

Direct-Transfer Rollover

When you leave a company and withdraw the funds from that company's 401(k) plan, the trustee will report your withdrawal on an IRS form 1099. If you can't show you put the money into a new plan, then you'll owe income taxes on the amount, plus a 10 percent penalty on the amount you withdrew before you were eligible.

Even if your transfer is being made by check, the former provider will make the check out to the new provider with an instruction to direct it to your new account. In practice, the check will be sent to you, and you'll mail it to the new plan provider. Because the check isn't in your name, it's still considered a direct transfer.

60-Day Rollover

If you decide to transfer your 401(k) using the 60-day rollover rule, the old provider will cut you a check in your name. You then have 60 days to redeposit the check into an IRA or your new 401(k) plan. If the old provider withholds taxes from the check it sends you, you must deposit the check plus the taxes they withheld into the new account. Otherwise the IRA views the taxes as a distribution, and you'll owe income tax as well as a 10 percent penalty on them. The disadvantages to the 60-day rollover are too severe to bother with if you're trying to protect your 401(k), and a very good reason to always stick with the direct transfer option.

> **Nest Eggs**
>
> It's a good idea to consolidate your 401(k) accounts if your new employer's plan offers good investment choices with low fees. If you don't like either your new plan or your old employer's plan, you can use the same direct trustee-to-trustee transfer to move your money to an IRA account that you manage yourself.

Withdrawing Early, When You're Out of Options

Many employers will allow loans and hardship withdrawals from the 401(k) partly because they don't want employees to hesitate to enroll in the first place for fear that their money will be completely inaccessible to them. The Summary Plan Document will outline the details of how the loan will work. Often the amount you can borrow is limited to 50 percent of the vested balance of your account. The loan isn't taxable and doesn't carry the 10 percent early withdrawal penalty unless you leave the employer and are not able to pay the loan back. In that case, there will be a short grace period before you have to restore the funds or the loan is considered a distribution and is taxable.

Loan payments are deducted from your pay pretax. The loan term and interest rate are up to the employer, but most will give a 5- or 10-year term with interest at the *prime rate* plus 1 or 2 percent. The interest is paid back to your account, less 1 or 2 percent as a fee for the loan.

def•i•ni•tion

The **prime rate** is the interest rate that commercial banks charge their best customers, generally large companies. It is lower than virtually all rates because the risk of default is very low.

Taking a loan against your 401(k) balance should be your last resort. The loan can hurt your account performance, and because the collateral amount that you're borrowing against is often held in a conservative account within your plan, your account may not perform as well as it would without the loan.

If your employer offers hardship withdrawals, you could be eligible for one if you have …

- An immediate and severe financial need, and the money isn't available from anyplace else.

- Already borrowed as much from the 401(k) plan as you're eligible, so a hardship withdrawal is the only option for getting money from the account.

You can use the money only for the following things, and you can't withdraw more than you need for the expense.

- Buying your primary home (not a vacation or second home).

- Paying 12 months' worth of college tuition, room and board, and fees for you, your spouse, your dependents, or children.

- Preventing foreclosure or eviction from your primary home.

◆ Paying tax-deductible medical expenses that will not be reimbursed by health insurance for you, your spouse, or your dependents.

Rainy Days

Many 401(k) plans offer loans and hardship withdrawals. Consider this important feature if you have only a small amount of liquid savings or a lot of debt. Roll the money from your previous employer's 401(k) plan into your new 401(k) to make the larger balance available in case of financial catastrophe.

You'll owe income tax but not the 10 percent penalty if you make a hardship withdrawal for these reasons:

◆ For income because you are permanently disabled.

◆ To pay medical debts that exceed 7.5 percent of your adjusted gross income.

◆ To comply with a court order, such as in a divorce.

◆ You retire between the ages of 55 and $59\frac{1}{2}$ and start a series of regular payments from the 401(k) based on an IRS formula and your life expectancy.

Unlike loans, hardship withdrawals are permanent. Once the money is out of the account, you can't put it back. The only alternative to rebuild the 401(k) is through regular contributions.

The Least You Need to Know

◆ If you don't yet have any savings built up, start setting aside your emergency fund while investing in your 401(k).

◆ An employer match is one of the best parts of a 401(k) and well worth adjusting your contribution in order to qualify for.

◆ The trustee-to-trustee direct transfer is by far the easiest and least risky of the rollover options.

◆ The best place to check the fees in your 401(k) investments is to refer to the prospectus or visit www.Morningstar.com.

◆ As your beneficiary situation changes, you must update the official beneficiary designations on your 401(k).

◆ Your 401(k) plan details are always available for you to review in the Summary Plan Document.

3

How They Work: IRA

In This Chapter

- ◆ How IRAs are different from other financial accounts
- ◆ Investments that work best
- ◆ Who can contribute and who can't
- ◆ Making contributions with withdrawals in mind
- ◆ Why Roth IRAs are amazing retirement accounts

Individual retirement accounts, which are almost universally referred to as IRAs, are the colored eggs in your nest egg basket. They're exciting because you get special breaks on your income taxes when you use them to save for retirement. In addition, unlike the retirement accounts you may have at work, you get to pick your IRA investments from an almost limitless number of choices. And of course, with such benefits comes responsibility. So let's learn the basics of how IRAs work, a little about the typical investments used in IRAs, and about the special tax-saving ways they help you build your retirement security. This chapter gives you the foundation you need to implement the IRA protection strategies we cover in this book.

Just the Facts

IRAs are great tax savers because the earnings in your account are tax-deferred until you withdraw them. That means every dollar stays invested—earning you returns—and is never withdrawn to pay taxes.

The special tax features of IRAs make them an entirely different breed of account from regular savings or plain investment accounts. These differences affect when you'll owe taxes on your account earnings and the tax rate you'll have to pay. To understand how this works, you need to understand a few tax terms:

- ◆ **Taxable income**   These are earnings from your job and from interest or dividends from your investments that you have to pay tax on each year.

- ◆ **Income tax rate**   This is the percentage of your income that you're required to pay to your local, state, or federal government. Tax rates are divided into brackets that start low for low-income earners and increase as one's income rises in a pattern that looks like an inverted pyramid.

Married, Filing Jointly

Tax Rate 2008	Taxable Income
35%	Income over $357,700
33%	$200,300 to $357,700
28%	$131,450 to $200,300
25%	$65,100 to $131,450
15%	$16,050 to $65,100
10%	Income up to $16,050

Rainy Days

In 2008, all states except Alaska, Florida, Nevada, New Hampshire, South Dakota, Tennessee, Texas, Washington, and Wyoming had income taxes that could affect withdrawals from your IRAs. In this book, we only deal with federal taxes, so check with your state revenue department to learn how state laws affect you and your accounts.

Single Filers

Tax Rate 2008	Taxable Income
35%	Income over $357,700
33%	$164,550 to $357,700
28%	$78,850 to $164,550
25%	$32,550 to $78,850
15%	$8,025 to $32,550
10%	Income up to $8,025

◆ **Marginal tax rate**   This is the rate on the highest bracket your income reached. Your marginal rate is the rate at which one extra dollar of new taxable income will be taxed. New income could include withdrawals that you make from your IRA, so knowing what their bracket is and how it affects you is important. For example, using the preceding tables, if you were a single filer in 2008 and had $45,000 in taxable income, your marginal tax rate would be 25 percent.

◆ **Adjusted gross income (AGI)**   AGI is calculated by adding your work income plus other income such as investment interest and dividends or alimony. From that total, subtract exclusions like alimony you paid and the cost of health insurance if you're self-employed. One reason you should know your AGI is to be sure you're eligible to make certain types of IRA contributions.

◆ **Capital gains tax rate**   This is the percentage of your investing profits that you must pay in taxes. If you sell an investment that you have held for a year or longer for more than you paid for it, you've made a profit or a capital gain. The tax law is written to encourage you to invest by making this tax rate lower than the rate you pay on income. For 2008, if your marginal tax bracket is 15 percent or less, then your capital gains rate is 0 percent. Taxpayers in the higher brackets pay a 15 percent capital gains rate, even though their income tax rate may be 25 percent or higher.

◆ **Tax-deferred account** Income or capital gains generated by investments in these accounts aren't taxable right away. They're deferred into the future, and taxes are often then owed on the amount withdrawn from the account.

◆ **Tax-deductible** When it relates to retirement accounts, tax-deductible means you get to reduce your taxable income by the amount you deposit in your retirement account/s. This doesn't reduce your tax liability dollar-for-dollar, but it is a big tax saver because it reduces the amount of income subject to your marginal tax bracket.

◆ **Contributions** The amount you deposit into your retirement account/s.

◆ **Withdrawals** The amount you take out of your retirement account/s.

◆ **Tax year** The rules controlling all retirement accounts including IRAs are based on tax years. This means your eligibility to contribute to an account is determined each year depending on a variety of factors, including your MAGI for the year and whether or not you have a retirement plan at work.

◆ **After-tax dollars** If your contribution to an IRA is made in after-tax dollars, it means you didn't get to deduct that amount from your taxable income. This could happen if you're ineligible to make deductible contributions to your Traditional IRA account (keep track of your contributions when you file your taxes with form 8606 in this case) or if you're contributing to a Roth account.

◆ **Pretax dollars** Investing pretax dollars means you can deduct the amount you deposited in the IRA from your taxable income. This money is "pretax" because getting the deduction means you haven't paid income taxes on those dollars yet—they're deferred.

When You Can Add to Your IRA

Retirement accounts can belong only to an individual. They can't be owned jointly by two people, and they can't be owned by a nonperson, like a trust. If you're married, each person can have an IRA and make a contribution to his account if:

- ◆ At least one spouse had taxable employment income for that tax year.

- ◆ The IRA account owner was younger than 70½ for the whole year.

Both spouses can contribute separately up to the IRA limit or their total earned income, whichever is less. If this seems like a lot to figure out, don't worry—the IRS gives you a little extra time to sort it all out. Although you can make contributions to your IRA throughout the year, you don't have to make final contributions until the tax deadline—April 15 of the following year or the next weekday if the 15th falls on a weekend.

> **Nest Eggs**
>
> Do you have a detailed question about IRAs or want to check into more specific examples? Check out IRS Publication 590 at www.irs.gov for all the specific rules regulating IRAs.

> **Rainy Days**
>
> Your annual contribution limit applies to all your IRA accounts, not each individual account if you have several. The IRS only limits total contributions; you'll be penalized for overcontributing, but you won't be penalized if you can't contribute up to the maximum allowed. If you discover you've overcontributed for the year, you won't be penalized if you withdraw the excess before you file your tax return.

IRA contributions are a use-it-or-lose-it proposition; you either make your contribution for the tax year or you don't. You can't deposit an amount this year that you were eligible to deposit for the previous tax year. To help you build your nest egg, the limits on what you can contribute annually are increasing, though. In 2008, you could deposit up to $5,000 into your IRA account. If you're age 50 or over, you can add a catch-up amount of $1,000 for a total of $6,000. Under current tax law, this catch-up amount is expected to stay level at $1,000 per year, while the basic contribution amount of $5,000 will be adjusted for inflation in 2009 and beyond.

To Deduct or Not to Deduct

Depending on your circumstances, you may be able to deduct the amount you put into your IRA account from income on your tax return. Whether or not you can take the deduction depends on your modified AGI and on whether you or your spouse had a plan at work. Modified AGI is your ordinary adjusted gross income, with a few adjustments that affect very few people. Following are the limits for 2008 that apply to single people and most married people. Check IRS publication 590 for updated limits for future years or for the limits if you're married but filing your tax return separately from your spouse.

How much can you deduct if you ARE covered by a plan at work?

If you're filing single, head of household, and your modified AGI is:

$53,000 or less	Full deduction
$53,001 to $63,000	Partial deduction
$63,001 or more	No deduction

If you're filing married, filing jointly, or qualifying widow(er), and your modified AGI is:

$85,000 or less	Full deduction
$85,001 to $105,000	Partial deduction
$105,001 or more	No deduction

How much can you deduct if you're NOT covered by a plan at work?

If you're filing single, head of household, qualifying widow(er), and your modified AGI is:

Any amount	Full deduction

If you're filing married, filing jointly, and spouse DOES NOT have a plan at work, and your modified AGI is:

Any amount	Full deduction

If you're filing married, filing jointly, and spouse DOES have a plan at work, and your modified AGI is:

$159,000 or less	Full deduction
$159,001 to $169,000	Partial deduction
$169,001 or more	No deduction

Withdrawal Time

You can withdraw money from your IRA anytime you want, but IRS rules encourage you to delay at least until you're older by putting an additional 10 percent penalty on withdrawals that are not "qualified."

The most common situations that would make an IRA withdrawal qualified are that you're:

- Age 59½ or older

- Disabled or you've died and your beneficiary is receiving the proceeds of your IRA

- Using your withdrawals to pay for college or other qualified higher education expenses

- Using a withdrawal or up to $10,000 toward a first-time home purchase

 Rainy Days

You can name a beneficiary who will collect the proceeds from your IRA when you die. It's important to keep your beneficiary designations up-to-date because IRA beneficiaries receive their inheritance regardless of what your will says.

When you do take IRA withdrawals, either qualified or not, at least a portion is taxed at income tax rates no matter whether the investments in the account grew because of interest or capital gains. What if you decide you like deferring your taxes and don't need the money in your IRA? Uncle Sam won't wait forever for you to start taking withdrawals and paying income taxes on your money. He mandates that you begin making withdrawals by April 1 following the year you turn 70½.

Getting Started: Opening and Investing Your IRA

Most financial institutions that sell investment vehicles like mutual funds and bank accounts provide IRA accounts to hold the investments in. The most common are banks and credit unions, mutual fund companies, insurance companies, and brokerage firms.

Each type of financial institution will have its own selection of investment vehicles to pick from. Which institution you choose depends on how well their investment selection allows you to pick investments that fit your target *asset allocation plan* and the investment cost. Chapter 7 will help you decide what asset allocation or investment you want.

def•i•ni•tion

An **asset allocation plan** works like an investment recipe for all your accounts. It dictates the percentage of your portfolio you'll invest in each asset class, such as stocks, bonds, and cash. How much of each class to target is determined by factors such as your age, your risk tolerance, and your investment goals.

When it's time to open your IRA, the financial institution you choose to work with will act as the account trustee. Many trustees charge an annual fee to maintain the IRA account, typically around $25, that may be waived once the IRA reaches a certain size.

Nest Eggs

Managing several individual IRAs with investments like stocks, mutual funds, or money market accounts in separate scattered accounts can get confusing. Brokerage firms like Fidelity Investments, the Vanguard Group, and Charles Schwab offer brokerage accounts that consolidate your separate investments into one account, which makes managing them easier.

The trustee also will give you the unavoidable paperwork. They'll give you an IRA adoption agreement and a plan document that describes the operational details of your account, which will include the types of allowable investments, contribution limits, and the process for making deposits and withdrawals. Your account is open once you sign the adoption agreement, which is usually part of the account application.

Predictably, the plan document is very long, but keep a copy to refer to and simply to have in your records. Most institutions maintain their documents on their website; saving an electronic copy will save you space and paper.

Rainy Days

The IRA is the holding account for the investments, not the investment itself. Sometimes the name an institution gives their IRA accounts imply that the IRA is the investment, too. If your bank calls the account an "IRA CD," remember that the two are separate. The certificate of deposit is the investment held within the IRA account.

You must make contributions in cash, usually via a check paid to the trustee. Common investments for IRAs are certificates of deposit, savings and money market accounts, mutual funds, annuities, and individual stocks and bonds.

- **Certificates of deposit** Like savings accounts, CDs also have FDIC insurance and can be bought from either a bank or a brokerage firm. CDs usually earn more interest than savings or money market accounts. Unlike savings and money market accounts, you can't move your money out of a CD any time you want. If you withdraw your money before the CD matures, you'll pay a penalty usually equal to a few months' interest.

- **Savings and money market accounts** These simple interest-earning accounts are available at banks, credit unions, or brokerage firms. They are a conservative IRA investment because their principal is often insured and they carry very low fees. You can move your money into or out of a savings or money market account and into another investment in your IRA anytime you want without a penalty.

- **Mutual funds** Mutual funds are a great investment option for IRAs because they offer stock and bond market investments without the hassle of having to pick individual stock or bond investments yourself. A mutual fund is a basket of individual investments—stocks, bonds, or even some cash—bundled together into one product. They are as risky or safe as the investments within them, so do your research and understand whether you're buying a risky mutual fund or a relatively safer one. You can open an IRA and invest in mutual funds by working directly with the mutual fund company or by buying the fund in your IRA brokerage account.

◆ **Annuities** Annuities come in two flavors, fixed and variable. Fixed annuities are a lot like certificates of deposit because they pay a fixed rate of interest that readjusts on a yearly basis. Some fixed annuities pay a higher teaser rate initially and then settle down to regular market rates for the remainder of their maturity period. Variable annuities are like mutual funds, containing a basket of individual stock or bond investments called subaccounts. These annuities change in value based on the performance of the investments in the subaccounts. Annuities are sold by life insurance companies and feature a life insurance component that increases their cost compared to a mutual fund and makes them tax-deferred, whether they are held in an IRA or not.

Any sales commissions or investment expenses inside your IRA reduce the value of your statutorily capped contributions and your investment's potential to grow. So avoid high investment expenses whenever you can. Annuities and some mutual funds carry high sales commissions and are bad investment choices for your IRA.

Rainy Days _____

IRAs can incur two types of fees, trustee fees and investment-related costs. The investment's prospectus outlines the investment fees, which can include sales commissions, management fees, and a "12-b1" marketing fee. Protect your IRA from fees by considering commission-free no-load mutual funds and by paying trustee fees out-of-pocket instead of having them withdrawn from your IRA.

Nurturing Your Nest Egg Before Retirement

Planning regular IRA contributions while you're still working is an important part of building retirement security. The reason is twofold. First, if you typically spend your whole paycheck, you'll get used to the lifestyle the whole check affords you, leaving no room for saving.

Second, if you're not saving for retirement, you have no hope of affording that lifestyle. Regular investing keeps your retirement lifestyle expectations reasonable and helps build the nest egg to support it when you stop working.

Most employer retirement plans (see Chapter 2) offer pre-tax contributions regardless of your income. This is a great benefit for tax savings now but can create tax issues after retirement. If your retirement income comes solely from Social Security or pension income, plus withdrawals from your retirement accounts, you could find yourself in the same high tax bracket in retirement that you were in when you were working. This could happen if your only source of cash in retirement is from taxable withdrawals from your retirement accounts. Since you deferred taxes when you contributed, Uncle Sam will want his share now that you're making withdrawals.

You can reduce this problem by adding nonretirement accounts to your long-term savings. These are just regular bank or mutual fund accounts that are not inside IRAs. With these accounts, you'll owe taxes on your earnings as you go—they're not tax-deferred—but in retirement you'd have cash available for lump-sum purchases without having to draw from your IRA and pay taxes.

 Rainy Days

Don't forget to file IRS form 8606 when you make nondeductible contributions to your IRA. When you retire, you—or your heirs—will be able to prove how much of your IRA balance is the money that you contributed after-tax—and is available to withdraw without additional tax—and how much is investment growth and is taxable income on withdrawal. If you missed a past year, you can file the Form 8606 late. There's a $50 penalty, but that's better than not getting the future tax break on your IRA withdrawals.

Contributing money to your IRA even when you can't deduct it on your tax return can be a good retirement income and good tax planning. Your contributions will help grow your nest egg, your investment growth is still tax-deferred until you withdraw money and—probably the biggest benefit—your non-deductible IRA will contain the principal contributions you made, called your IRA basis, that you can withdraw tax-free in retirement. The amount you contribute to your IRA but don't get to deduct is called your "IRA basis." When you take money out of your IRA to pay for retirement living expenses, you don't pay tax on it again. You only pay tax on the money that was earned by the investments, not on the dollars you originally contributed. You still pay income tax rates on your withdrawal, but because part of your withdrawal is tax-free, your overall tax cost will be lower.

Roth IRA

Roth IRAs—named after the former Senate Finance Committee Chairman William V. Roth Jr.—have amazing tax benefits. While you don't get to deduct the money you contribute to them, their greatest advantage is that when you make withdrawals, none of the money is taxable—neither your basis nor the earnings in your account! Instead of being tax-deferred accounts like regular IRAs, Roth IRA withdrawals are essentially tax-free. Of course you didn't get a break on your deposit, but you're not paying tax on your earnings. And they can stay tax-free and continue to grow for a long time. Unlike regular IRAs, you don't have to start taking money out of your Roth after you turn age 70½. If you don't need the money, you can leave it in the Roth IRA as long as you want.

Of course, such an amazing IRA is going to have limitations, and here they are.

- ◆ You can only contribute a limited amount into your Roth IRA, and that amount is reduced by any contributions you made to your regular IRA. In 2008, total IRA contributions were limited to $5,000. So if you put $3,000 in your regular IRA, you can only put $2,000 in your Roth IRA. Current tax law says that this limit will increase in increments of $500 each year, so in 2009 you can put $5,500 in your IRA and in 2010 you can deposit $6,000. Roth IRAs have the same catch-up provision as regular IRAs. If you're over age 50, you can put in an extra $1,000.

- ◆ You can also contribute to a Roth IRA only if you make less than a certain amount of income. Tax penalties for contributing to a Roth IRA when you're not eligible are steep. If your MAGI is below the bottom of the range in the following table, you can make the full Roth IRA contribution. If your income is inside the range, then your contribution amount is reduced—called phasing out your contribution. The phase-out is gradual, so once your income reaches the top of the range, you're not eligible to contribute at all.

Tax Filing Status 2008 Income Phase-Out Range

Tax Status	Phase-Out Range
Married, filing jointly or head of household	$159,000 to $169,000
Single	$101,000 to $116,000
Married, filing separately	$0 to $10,000

Not all contributions to your Roth IRA have to come from annual contributions. You can also convert money from your Traditional IRA into a Roth IRA. You're eligible to convert regular IRA money to your Roth in a tax year that your MAGI is greater than $100,000. This AGI limit applies to everyone except married taxpayers who are filing separately. If you're filing single, married filing jointly, or filing as head of household, you can convert as long as your income is below $100,000. If you're married filing separately, you can't convert your IRA to a Roth IRA at all.

Full Account

Be careful to check the Roth IRA eligibility limits. The penalties are steep if you contribute when the rules prohibit it. Check your MAGI each year before you contribute to make sure you're within the limit. Tax preparers won't usually ask about Roth IRA eligibility, because that information doesn't factor into your tax return in any way. Your investment company won't usually ask, either, because all they need to know is what year you want the deposit applied for. Recently, I've found several accounts where the investor made the deposit without realizing he was ineligible. If this happens to you, you can take back the excess contribution before you file your taxes without a problem. If you've already filed your return, there's a process to follow with the IRS to withdraw the excess and pay the penalties. An acquaintance once told me that his tax preparer recommended ignoring the mistake "because no one checks." That's bad advice! Straighten out your mistake, even by paying a penalty, so you won't have the threat of bigger penalties later hanging over your head.

Check the resources section at the back of the book for online calculators to help you decide whether a Roth conversion makes sense for you. You'll owe income taxes on the amount of money you convert because all Roth contributions must be with after-tax money. Even after this additional cost, conversion may still be a good idea if you have more than 10 years before you'll start withdrawals; you want to defer withdrawals well past age 70; or you believe your tax bracket in retirement will be at least as high as while you're working. We have more on how to decide whether to convert your IRA to a Roth in Chapter 10.

You can withdraw money you contributed to your Roth IRA at any time. After all, you contributed it after-tax, so there's no tax on the withdrawal. In order for your or your heir's withdrawals to be tax- and penalty-free, they must qualify by meeting at least one of these key tests plus an additional five-year rule:

♦ Made after you turn age 59½

♦ Made after you died

♦ Made after you become disabled, as the IRS defines it

♦ Made to pay for permitted first-time home-buyer expenses

The five-year rule is applied differently to earnings from Roth IRA contributions and earnings from Roth conversions. The rule for contributions says that your eventual withdrawal isn't qualified unless you've waited to withdraw for at least five tax years since your first deposit. That means if you make your first Roth contribution in the 2008 tax year, you will meet your five-year rule by the end of 2013. The five-year rule only applies once, so once you've run the five-year course with your first Roth IRA contribution, you don't have to worry about waiting for subsequent contributions to age.

Nest Eggs _____

You may not have to wait five full calendar years to make a Roth withdrawal. Remember that tax years are the same as calendar years, but you get a grace period until tax day of the following year to make your Roth IRA contribution. So if you make your first Roth IRA contribution April 15, 2009, for the 2008 tax year, you'll meet your five-year rule December 31, 2013, not quite a full five calendar years later.

Roth conversions are a little trickier. Each conversion starts its own five-year rule countdown, but if you first opened your Roth account with a conversion, the conversion can also start the one-time clock for contributions.

The Least You Need to Know

+ April 15, or tax day, is the deadline to make IRA contributions.

+ You must start making withdrawals at age 70½ from your IRAs, including Traditional, SEP, and SIMPLE but excluding Roth.

+ Eligibility rules may change each year, so check the rules each year before contributing to your account.

+ Keep track of nondeductible IRA contributions on tax form 8606.

+ Don't use investments with high fees in your IRA.

+ The annual contribution limit for IRAs applies to all your IRA accounts combined, including Roths.

4

Special Employer Plans

In This Chapter

- ♦ Plans for self-employed people and small businesses that rival the 401(k) plans big companies have
- ♦ How plans for government and nonprofit employees work
- ♦ Tips to decide if a Roth 401(k) is for you
- ♦ Knowing when your plan assets are at risk

Individual retirement accounts and 401(k) plans are not the only games in town. If you work for a small employer, are self-employed, or work for the government or a nonprofit organization, special plans are available for you that are similar to—and in many ways better than—the 401(k).

The tax code tries to make it possible for everyone to save in a tax-favored way for retirement—no matter where he works. Understanding how each of these special retirement plans works will help you decide which is best for you and how each fits into your plan for retirement security.

Plans for the Small Business and the Self-Employed

Just because your business is small doesn't mean your retirement plan has to be. Small businesses and self-employed people have three amazing retirement plan options whose benefits rival those of the big, expensive-to-administer 401(k) plans. Two of the plans use regular IRA accounts with special benefits to mimic the behavior of a 401(k) but without the cost. One is called the Savings Incentive Match Plan for Employees or the SIMPLE plan. The other is called the Simplified Employee Pension or SEP plan. The third option, called the single-person 401(k) or the solo 401(k), simplifies the administration of a 401(k) enough to make it affordable for single-person companies and mom-and-pop shops.

It's Really SIMPLE

If you work for a small company, you might already have a SIMPLE plan. SIMPLEs are common in companies with 30 or fewer employees, but companies with up to 100 employees are eligible to open them. Under a SIMPLE plan, your employer opens a SIMPLE IRA account for you—or asks you to open one yourself—and then both you and the employer can make contributions. SIMPLE IRAs are available at a variety of financial service firms, but use a mutual fund or brokerage account for your SIMPLE IRA to be sure you have the best selection of low-cost investments for your account.

Money in your SIMPLE IRA—whether you deposit it or your employer does—vests immediately, meaning it is 100 percent yours right away and is separate from the employer's assets. This means there's no waiting for the employer match to vest as in a 401(k) account. And, like a 401(k) account, your money is safe from the employer's creditors if the employer goes out of business. For the 2008 tax year, you can defer up to $10,500 of your pay. You can defer an additional $2,500 more if you are over age 50 by the end of the calendar year. For 2009 and beyond, like most other retirement plan limitations, these limits will increase with inflation. Check IRS Publication 560, "Retirement Plans for Small Business," for updates.

Your employer must either match what you deposit up to 3 percent of your pay or make an automatic 2 percent contribution to everyone's account, whether or not the employee contributes himself. This mandatory match, like the required match in a 401(k) plan, is part of ensuring the SIMPLE plan benefits all employees regardless of pay.

Think of your SIMPLE IRA as a turbocharged IRA account that allows higher contributions than regular IRAs. As IRAs, they have the same withdrawal limitations and rules that regular IRAs have, including the 10 percent penalty for withdrawals before you turn 59½ years old. Plus, if you make that withdrawal before your SIMPLE IRA is two years old, the 10 percent penalty is increased to 25 percent. You can roll over a SIMPLE IRA to your regular IRA when you leave your job. If you're the employer, you can close a SIMPLE IRA by letting your employees know by October 1 of the last year of the plan that you're closing the plan.

Nest Eggs

Even if your employer opens a SIMPLE IRA account for you, you can still pick your own SIMPLE IRA investments by moving money from your employer's account into a personal SIMPLE account. This is a great benefit of a SIMPLE plan, allowing you to choose virtually any investment you want.

Rainy Days

If you're an employer with a lot of employee turnover, you can limit who's eligible for the SIMPLE plan, therefore limiting the amount you have to contribute to their accounts. You can exclude employees who made less than $5,000 in either of the previous two years or who are not expected to make $5,000 this year from the plan.

Employers like SIMPLE plans because they're easier and cheaper to administer than 401(k) plans. There's no separate plan document to prepare; for example, IRS forms 5304-SIMPLE or 5305-SIMPLE are already written and approved. And SIMPLE IRA accounts are available at most mutual fund or brokerage firms. No discrimination testing is used to ensure the plan is fair to all employees because of the required 3 percent match or 2 percent automatic employer contribution. The brokerage or mutual fund company will do the IRS reporting on the SIMPLE IRA accounts for you for at most a small annual fee per account.

> **Rainy Days**
>
> Minimize the fees in your retirement account as much as possible. If your employer doesn't pay your annual SIMPLE IRA account fee, you should pay it with a separate check to your mutual fund or brokerage firm instead of having the fee—usually only $25 or less—deducted from your account balance.

SIMPLE 401(k) Plans

SIMPLE 401(k) plans combine the features of SIMPLE IRAs and regular 401(k)s. SIMPLE 401(k)s have the contribution limits and employer match rules of SIMPLE plans. Employees' accounts are 100 percent vested immediately. Employers can limit eligibility more strictly for the SIMPLE 401(k) than the SIMPLE IRA. They can require that individuals be at least age 21 and have given at least a year of service or 1,000 hours in order to be eligible. SIMPLE 401(k)s can also allow loans and hardship withdrawals like regular 401(k)s.

SEP IRAs

Any company can choose to offer a SEP as their retirement plan, but SEP plans are especially popular with people who are self-employed and who don't have employees. Unlike SIMPLE plans, 100 percent of the contributions comes from the employer; employees don't contribute to a SEP plan. Contribution limits are higher than SIMPLE plans permit, which allows a self-employed person to maximize what he's investing into his account. Because he doesn't have employees to contribute for, 100 percent of the company contribution goes into his own account.

Like the SIMPLE plan, SEPs use an IRA account for each worker. Total SEP contributions can be as much as 25 percent of the employee's pay up to $46,000 for the 2008 tax year—or if he's self-employed, up to 25 percent of his net income after expenses. This could be much more than the $10,500 plus inflation adjustments limit a SIMPLE plan allows. SEP contributions can be made up until the employee files his tax return for the year.

Rainy Days

If you contribute more than you're allowed in one tax year, you'll owe penalties and have to withdraw the excess. If you have self-employment income and contribute to a SEP plan, you can also contribute to a regular IRA and an employer's 401(k). If you have more than one 401(k), you can't contribute the maximum to both. Check with your CPA to be sure you're doing it right!

SEP IRAs are easy to open and are available in all the same places you can open regular IRAs and SIMPLE IRAs. Because employees are not contributing, you have a little more flexibility in starting a plan and making contributions. You don't need to give employees a 90-day notice of plan changes as you do with a SIMPLE plan. In fact, you can wait up until the due date of your company tax return before deciding how much to contribute to the SEP. IRS Form 5305-SEP, available online, can serve as your plan document. You need to give a copy to your employees, if you have them, every year; but if it's just you in the plan, you only need to keep a copy on file. There's nothing to file with the IRS.

Nest Eggs

If you own a small business with employees, the SIMPLE IRA or SIMPLE 401(k) plan will probably work better for you than the SEP because it's funded mostly with employee contributions. If you're on your own without employees, the higher contribution limits of the SEP or the Solo 401(k) will let you contribute more pretax for retirement and save more taxes.

If you have employees and decide to use a SEP plan anyway, as with the SIMPLE, contributions to the SEP are 100 percent vested immediately and can be moved to another IRA account anytime after being deposited in the original SEP IRA account.

SEP contributions don't need to be made every year, but they do need to benefit all workers at your company equally when you do make them.

You must contribute the same percentage of pay into everyone's SEP account as you do your own, and you need to include anyone age 21 or older who's been an employee in three of the past five years.

Solo 401(k)

If you're self-employed with no employees other than your spouse and you're anxious to contribute as much as you can to your retirement plan, the new Solo 401(k)—also called a Self-Employed 401(k)—may work even better for you than the SEP IRA. Solo 401(k) plans have all the bells and whistles of regular 401(k) plans, including the high contribution limits and options to take loans. Like regular 401(k) plans, both the employee and the employer contribute to the plan. Because you're a solo operation, this means you sit in both seats. As an employee, you can contribute up to the 401(k) limit for the year—plus the extra catch-up if you're at least age 50 before year-end. As the employer, you can add a profit-sharing contribution to the account that is as much as 25 percent of your income. Total contributions are capped at $47,000 for 2009 and will increase with inflation each year. You have until the tax return is due to make your deposit. The employee part of the contribution isn't based on a percentage of your income, so you may be able to contribute more to a Solo 401(k) than you can to a SEP.

Even though it's just you in the plan and maybe your spouse—if she's involved in your business—you still have to follow all the regular 401(k) rules. Your brokerage or mutual fund company will guide you in what you have to do, but in the end you're responsible for the plan being managed correctly. As the plan administrator, you're responsible for the following things:

◆ Making sure you always have a current copy of the plan document available in your file.

◆ Filing annual tax report form 5500 once the plan grows beyond $250,000.

◆ Calculating how much you and your spouse can deposit in the account and what the profit-sharing and match amounts are.

Don't shirk your responsibilities as plan administrator. 401(k) plans have more fun features than IRAs to save you tax money, but you must follow their more stringent rules. If you don't follow the rules, your plan could be disqualified, making the money in the plan taxable immediately. These requirements may make the Solo 401(k) a hassle to work with, but if your business is growing and successful, it may be worth it for both the tax savings on your contributions and the chance to build your retirement nest egg.

403(b) Plans: More Than 401(k)s for Teachers

If you work in a public school system, a nonprofit organization, or in the clergy, you may have a 403(b) plan at work. These special accounts might resemble 401(k) accounts with a nonprofit twist, but 403(b) accounts were available long before 401(k)s appeared. The IRS created 403(b)s in 1958 to provide a mechanism for public employees to save toward retirement. Twenty years later, employees of private companies gained access to 401(k) accounts.

403(b)s are much like 401(k)s, but because they were created before all the restrictions of ERISA were created, they don't have all the same rules and restrictions that 401(k)s do. If you do work for a nonprofit, have a 403(b), and your employer contributes to your plan, you may have the unusual circumstances of having a 403(b) that is subject to ERISA.

403(b)s are identical to 401(k)s in that:

- Contributions to the account are pretax.

- You will pay penalties for taking money out of the account before age 59½.

- Money in the account is tax-deferred until you withdraw it, then it's taxed as income.

- You must start making minimum withdrawals from the account at age 70½.

- You're responsible for choosing the investments.

- They can allow loans and hardship withdrawals.

403(b)s differ from 401(k)s in that:

◆ Employers don't usually contribute to 403(b) accounts.

◆ In most cases, 403(b)s aren't subject to the stringent ERISA rules that 401(k)s are, so they are cheaper for an employer to maintain than 401(k)s.

◆ Not being under ERISA means that employees are even more personally responsible for choosing investments that have low fees and are good for their retirement plans. Employers often make this choice easier by offering more than one 403(b) vendor for the employees to choose from.

Full Account

If you've had a 403(b) for a while, you probably have an assortment of different accounts with different investment companies. I once had a client who could choose among more than twenty 403(b) providers! It's understandable how accounts can get out of hand when you have that many choices.

Recent rules should start to reduce the number of choices you'll have for new plans, but you still need to consolidate all your old 403(b) accounts. Start by checking the fees and investment choices of each. High expenses are an account killer, and you need a good selection—at least 10 funds total—of both stock and bond funds in the account you decide to use.

If you have an old account through an insurance company, check the annuity surrender value. Once the surrender value equals, or gets close to, the current value, it will probably be worth transferring to a less expensive account. TIAA-CREF 403(b)s are invested in annuities, but they're on the "good guy" list; they have low fees and good investment choices.

The 403(b)'s Partner: 401(a) Plans

Many lucky employees who have 403(b) accounts that they contribute to also have 401(a) accounts for their employer's contributions. In this case, 401(a) accounts look a lot like 403(b) accounts except only the employer contributes to the 401(a). Nonprofits pair the 401(a) plan with a 403(b) plan so they can provide the employee benefit of matching employee contributions. Employees contribute to the 403(b) and the employer either matches their contributions by contributing to the 401(a) account or contributes an automatic amount in the 401(a) whether or not the employee contributes to the 403(b).

Here are a few facts about 401(a) plans:

- ◆ 401(a) plans are special because employers can set up different plans for different groups of employees, such as managers or unionized workers.

- ◆ Employers can allow loans against vested 401(a) balances and hardship withdrawals.

- ◆ 401(a)s can have cliff or graded vesting schedules just like 401(k)s. This means that an employee may need to work at the company for a couple of years before she completely owns the plan balance.

- ◆ Like other retirement accounts, the employee will owe a 10 percent penalty if she withdraws money from her account before age $59\frac{1}{2}$, and she must start taking minimum distributions once she is age $70\frac{1}{2}$.

457 Deferred-Compensation Plans

457 plans are often called deferred-compensation or deferred comp plans because employees are deferring their pay by making contributions into the plan. Yes, this is also the case with all the other types of retirement plans, including the 401(k) and SIMPLE plans we've already told you about. But for whatever reason, 457 plans are the ones that have taken the "deferred comp" moniker.

There are two types of 457 plans: 457(b) plans and 457(f) plans. In general, state and local governments provide 457(b) plans while large, tax-exempt organizations like hospitals and universities run 457(f) plans, usually for their upper management employees.

457(b) plans are different than 401(k) plans and other similar retirement plans in that:

- ◆ They don't carry the 10 percent penalty if an employee withdraws his money before he turns age $59\frac{1}{2}$.

- ◆ They don't need to be offered to all employees of the organization.

◆ Contribution limits are the same as 401(k)s up until an employee is within three years of the plan's normal retirement age. At this point, the "last three rule" takes effect, doubling the maximum allowable contribution he can make.

457(b) plans work a lot like 401(k) plans, including:

◆ The employee makes pretax contributions.

◆ The employer may contribute to the plan and assign a vesting schedule to its contributions.

◆ Minimum distributions must start by the time the employee is age 70½.

◆ An employee can access his balance through hardship withdrawals.

◆ An employee can roll over his plan to another plan if he changes employers.

Nest Eggs

You don't have to be an employee of the organization to participate in its 457 plan. Unlike 403(b)s and 401(k)s, independent contractors can participate in the organization's 457 plan where they work.

457(f) plans are sophisticated employee benefit plans that are most often used to attract and retain high-level executives. They have the amazing benefit of having very high or unlimited contribution limits, but the catch is that the assets in the plan must always be at risk of forfeiture. This means that the money in your 457 plan remains subject to your employer's creditors; your account isn't protected like a 401(k) or a SIMPLE IRA. This substantial risk of forfeiture is a critical part of the plan because once the assets are no longer at risk, they become taxable as income. We've included the basics next, but carefully review your 457(f) plan with your employer and an independent financial or tax advisor before deciding to participate.

◆ A vesting schedule outlines when the compensation in the plan becomes available to the employee.

◆ Once the plan is vested, the executive is entitled to the assets in the plan, as long as she continues with the company until a future specified retirement date.

◆ The benefits of the plan may be taxable once they vest. Many employers make extra payments to their executives to offset the cost of the tax.

Employer Roths: Roth 401(k) and Roth 403(b)

Roth 401(k) and 403(b) accounts make the great long-term tax savings of Roth IRAs available to employees lucky enough to have this option without the income eligibility restrictions of Roth IRAs. Just as with a Roth IRA, an employee's deposit into a Roth employer account doesn't save him any income taxes right away—deposits are made after-tax—but account earnings are tax-free. In fact, the only great feature of the Roth IRA that Roth employer accounts are missing is the option to defer withdrawals forever.

Remember, with a Roth IRA, a person doesn't have to start withdrawing money from his account when he turns age 70½ like one does with a regular IRA. However, Roth employer accounts require minimum distributions just like regular IRAs starting at age 70½. Fortunately, the withdrawals are tax-free, and if you'd like to avoid the required distribution rules altogether, you can transfer your Roth employer account to a Roth IRA, as long as you're not working for the employer anymore and the IRS hasn't closed this loophole by the time you get to that age.

The Roth employer account will offer you the option to make both pre-tax contributions to the regular 401(k) or 403(b) account side of the plan and after-tax contributions to the Roth side. This is a great benefit to tax planning because you can decide how much you want to deposit into each side of the account.

But the Roth employer plan is still only one account and not both a regular employer plan plus a Roth plan. You can't deposit up to the IRS limit into both sides of the account. For instance, if the IRS limit that year is $20,500, then you have the choice to count all of your deposit toward the Roth and none toward the regular 401(k) or 403(b) account or apply part to the Roth and part to the regular plan. You can't deposit

$20,500 to each option. Remember, like the Roth IRA, you'll miss out on the tax deduction now, but you'll have a great source of tax-free income once you retire.

Nest Eggs

I really like Roth 401(k) and Roth 403(b) accounts. I know that deposits are made after-tax and that getting the tax deduction goes a long way toward making the retirement plan deposits affordable. But if you think ahead to retirement, you're going to be thrilled to have tax-free income available—especially if tax rates are higher than they are now, an unfortunate likelihood.

The only disappointing feature about Roth plans through work is that you still have the same contribution limit—you have to split your deposit between the two accounts or pick one or the other. I suggest you back into this decision by making sure you're building tax-deferred accounts (like your regular 401[k]), as well as tax-free accounts like the Roth and taxable accounts like savings and regular nonretirement investment accounts. Having a variety of accounts to draw from gives you flexibility in retirement to pay for large or nonmonthly expenses, like cars and vacations, without having to draw taxable income from your tax-deferred accounts. If you don't have money growing in tax-free Roth accounts, this is a good opportunity to start.

The Least You Need to Know

- ◆ IRS rules restrict account withdrawals until age 59½.

- ◆ You must start making withdrawals from most plans starting at age 70½.

- ◆ Investment vehicles, such as lower-cost mutual funds in your retirement accounts, can help avoid high annuities costs.

- ◆ Get clear tax and financial advice from an independent advisor before contributing to a 457 plan.

Part 2

Tending Your Nest Egg

Once you have the basics, it's time to start applying your knowledge. Here, you'll learn how to begin your nest egg and keep it growing. Once you decide how much to invest and what to invest it in, we'll tell how to keep it all balanced no matter what happens in the economy or in your life. You find ideas on building the nest egg while you're raising kids and changing jobs. These chapters offer help if you're faced with dipping into your accounts because of a financial hardship or divorce and give advice as you start rebuilding your accounts again.

"Sometimes I just like to check in and see how it's doing."

Chapter 5

Going Online for Help

In This Chapter

- ◆ Using online account aggregators to keep track of retirement accounts

- ◆ When to believe what retirement calculators are telling you

- ◆ Selecting the best calculators

- ◆ Adjusting goals or annual savings to make retirement achievable

- ◆ Double-checking calculations with a fee-only financial planner

Over the years, you'll probably accumulate a variety of work retirement plans and IRA accounts. Keeping them organized and on track to building a nest egg that's organized and well invested can become a bit of a challenge, but fortunately there are easy-to-use, and free, tools online to help.

Once you've organized your accounts, figuring out how much you need and how much to save is the next challenge. The Internet comes to the rescue to help with this. What used to take math-ematically skilled financial planners hours using pencil and paper or software spreadsheets is now accessible to even the most math-phobic individual through online calculators.

However, online retirement planning tools are like many other computer calculators—if you enter worthless numbers in the form of unrealistic expectations and assumptions, you'll get worthless numbers out. Knowing whether you have the right number when you're done, and how those results affect your savings plan, is a critical part of building a secure retirement nest egg.

Keeping It Organized

Setting up online access to your financial accounts is a great way to stay organized and keep track of a multitude of details and accounts. When you first access your accounts on the web, they may be listed under pretty mundane names—for example, 401(k), company savings plan, Traditional IRA, or even just IRA. Many sites will let you nickname your accounts by adding to or replacing their default names completely.

 Nest Eggs

Keeping IRA accounts that have pre-tax contributions—contributions that you took a deduction for on your tax return—separate from IRAs with after-tax contributions will help keep track of how much of the withdrawal you'll owe tax on. Don't forget to also file form 8606 in each tax year that you make nondeductible contributions.

This is a great way to get organized, especially if you want to earmark an account for a special purpose, such as vacation fund or early retirement fund. You can also use nicknames to keep track of important features of the account, such as whether an IRA has any after-tax contributions in it. By naming the account "Nondeductible IRA," you'll remember you made contributions that were not deductible on your tax return that year because they were made after-tax.

Many brokerage websites will let you see the accounts of other people who have given you permission to access their information, including elder parents whose finances you might be managing or monitoring. If you're overseeing the accounts for your household, having your spouse give you access will allow you to see both his and your own accounts on one web page. For instance, Fidelity Investments calls this feature inquiry access on its site. If the site also has asset allocation tools like Fidelity's has, having the household's accounts on one page will allow you to easily check the asset allocation of all accounts combined.

Managing the proliferation of accounts that can accumulate is important. Consolidating your retirement accounts into as few separate accounts as possible will help you keep this part of your finances organized. Combine previous employer plans into an IRA account or your current employer plan. Rolling your SEP or SIMPLE plan into an IRA

Nest Eggs

Many mutual funds and brokerage firms waive their annual fee for accounts that meet minimum balances. Combining accounts using one brokerage firm not only helps organize but also helps reduce the fees you pay.

if you're no longer self-employed or working for the employer who offered the plan will minimize the accounts you have to keep track of. Using a brokerage firm instead of multiple banks or mutual fund accounts will reduce the number of accounts you have to track. With a brokerage account, you won't need a new retirement account for each individual investment you own.

Online *account aggregators* like www.Yodlee.com will help keep track of your accounts even if they are at separate financial institutions. After you've linked your accounts to the aggregator and entered the online user name and password for each account, the aggregator copies the information from the individual financial sites and presents it as a list of accounts on a single web page. No more clicking around a handful of browser windows trying to make sense of scattered account information, not to mention a flurry of user names and passwords. Many brokerage firms and banks use aggregators like Yodlee to provide similar services on their own websites.

def•i•ni•tion

Account aggregators are free online services that help you organize your accounts and track your expenses. They make finding the "don't really need" parts of your budget easy and will give you pie charts to help analyze your spending patterns. Be sure to read the security information on the site, and never access your financial information from an unsecured Internet connection.

Most financial account websites make statements for the last couple of years available online. But don't rely only on the site to keep your archive; always keep a separate copy of each regular monthly or quarterly statement and then a copy of the year-end statement for each of your retirement accounts. If the year-end statement shows the activity for the year, including deposits and withdrawals, you can discard or delete the periodic statements and just keep the final year-end tally.

Nest Eggs

Many brokerage firms offer a way to consolidate the account statements of everyone in the household into one combined paper statement. Check the customer service link on their website to see if your broker offers this "account householding."

If you prefer to keep paper statements as a backup to your electronic files, store the statements with your tax returns or in a separate notebook organized by account. Be sure you have a record of your contributions and withdrawals and especially any after-tax contributions you made to your IRA or employer's retirement plan. These nondeductible contributions establish what's known as a "basis" in your account—the initial price you paid for an investment before it has grown in value in your portfolio. When you make withdrawals, you're entitled to take out as much as the basis without paying additional tax. If you lose track of these special contributions, you could ultimately pay too much income tax in retirement.

Helpful Tools

Account aggregators are not only a big help in tracking account balances, but they help project retirement expenses as well. Not everyone tracks his expenses closely enough to know off the top of his head what his retirement expenses might be. Some people are fortunate enough to have a salary and spending habits that fit naturally together. This doesn't necessarily mean that they have a super high income—in fact, it could mean they're very conscientious spenders—it just means that the amount they want to spend fits comfortably within their means. These folks aren't stressed about covering their monthly bills so they don't track their expenses. This can make retirement planning something of a shot in the dark for them because without knowing how much life costs now, it's difficult to project what retirement expenses might be.

This is where online account aggregators can be a big help. The aggregator can easily interpret online banking and credit and debit card transactions and automatically assign them into an expense category. If you use online banking or a credit card for most of your spending transactions, instead of using cash or writing a paper check, an aggregator like Mint.com, Wesabe (www.wesabe.com), or an aggregator provided on your bank website will give you a ballpark idea of your total expenses and how they fall into basic categories, such as housing, utilities, groceries, and entertainment.

Once you have a good idea of the monthly retirement income need you're shooting for, you can start compiling the rest of the assumptions you'll use in your retirement projection. You need to consider these three basic ones.

- Inflation: Most online calculators will automatically assume inflation to be between 3 and 4 percent. Historically, inflation has averaged just over 3 percent in the United States, but many economists expect it to be higher in the future. Where the calculator asks you to enter a projected inflation rate, use at least 4 percent.

- Portfolio returns: Most online calculators ask you to assume a flat annual return for your portfolio. Some will allow you to use two different rates: one for before retirement and one to represent the portfolio return after retirement, when it's invested in, presumably, less-aggressive, lower-return investments. A good rule of thumb is to assume the portfolio will return 3 percent more than your inflation projection while you're working and 1 percent more than inflation after retirement, if the calculator allows it. If the calculator only allows one number, try the calculation with a return 2 percent higher than inflation.

- Life expectancy: Many people scoff at financial planners who want their clients to plan for a long retirement. It may be hard to think of yourself at a very advanced age, but it's important to plan for your money to live a long time—at least as long as you will. After all, you may only expect to live to age 85, but you certainly don't want to spend your 84th birthday wondering how you're going to live when you only have one more year of expenses in your bank account and you're physically feeling pretty peppy. Assume a life

expectancy of at least age 95, and preferably 100, in your retirement projections. This will reduce the chances that you'll save too
little and virtually eliminate the chance that you'll outlast your
resources. It will also give you a little bit of wiggle room if your
expenses end up being higher than you expected.

Rainy Days _____

These basic assumptions will help you get a rough estimate of how
much money you'll need in retirement and whether you're on track
to make it work. Financial planners have access to—and know how to
use—much more sophisticated planning calculators. If you're within 20
years of retiring, it's a good idea to check your numbers against theirs at
least every couple of years.

Comparing the Online Calculators

A quick Google web search will generate a huge list of online retirement calculators. Look for one that doesn't require you to register or
surrender any personal contact information to use the site. Stick with
calculators that are housed within independent websites not related to
a financial services company. But if you decide to use the calculator on
your broker's site, check the results against a couple of other calculators
to see if the results differ. If the site has an incentive to encourage you
to save, it may have assumptions within the calculators that are unrea-
sonably conservative.

Whichever calculator you ultimately decide to rely on, it should only
produce final figures that illustrate how much you need to save or how
much you need to accumulate to retire; it shouldn't generate recommendations to buy a specific financial product or invest in a particular
investment scheme. Should you find yourself facing a financial sales
pitch at the conclusion of the calculator process, close the site and
start the process again with another calculator that appears to be more
independent.

To begin your online calculation, make a quick dry-run with rough
numbers to get an idea of how the calculator works and what information you need. Next, gather any information you were missing during

your test run, and repeat the calculation with more accurate numbers. Print the result so you can compare it to other calculators.

Most calculators only allow fixed-rate assumptions for portfolio return and inflation to make the calculator easier to use. This means your calculations are based on the assumption that inflation and investment returns will be the same each year. Because real-life portfolio returns and inflation are never the same every year, the trade-off for calculator simplicity is that your projection is more of a ballpark estimate than bull's-eye accurate.

The more sophisticated calculators apply Monte Carlo analysis to their results to estimate the likelihood the calculated result will come true. A calculator with Monte Carlo programming runs a formula similar to the ones the basic calculators use and then projects a Monte Carlo estimate of the probability of that outcome. To arrive at this probability, the Monte Carlo simulation runs through the retirement calculation thousands of times, each time relying on a different rate for portfolio return and inflation. The result of the Monte Carlo simulation will be the number of those repeated calculations that were successful— meaning the probability that you had enough money to retire or the probability that saving as much as you've calculated will meet your goal, depending on the analysis you were running and the information you put into the calculator.

One popular online Monte Carlo calculator is at www. FlexibleRetirementPlanner.com. This complex calculator lets you distinguish between taxable and tax-deferred retirement assets, as well as tax-free assets such as Roth IRA accounts. You can also change variables such as income tax rate, and you can assume changes in spending during retirement. This calculator generates a measure of the probability that your scenario will result in a financially comfortable retirement based on the retirement assets you will have, the time you'll probably live, and the economic conditions you'll encounter. The level of detail in the variables you'll submit to this calculator gives you a more accurate projection if you put in the right information. Unfortunately, with more detailed input comes a higher likelihood you could make a mistake that will dramatically alter your results. Compare this result with a non-Monte Carlo result to see if you're in the ballpark.

Nest Eggs _____

If you're planning to have a retirement job, it's helpful to use a calculator that lets you input the projected income from that job in addition to pension or Social Security income. Check out the calculator at www.AARP.com/money if you're planning to work after retirement.

A web search for retirement calculators will uncover many sites that use the basic calculators developed by KJE Computer Solutions, LLC (www.DinkyTown.net) or CalcXML LLC (www.CalcXML.com). KJE Computer's calculators incorporate an online technology tool that makes it easy to see how changing a variable, such as portfolio return or inflation, will affect your result. These calculators are fun to use and a good way to learn more about how small adjustments can change a plan. CalcXML's programs take the input in one table and then present the results with a bar chart and a table. The worksheet stays accessible at the top of the page so you can make changes and rerun it. Try running a version of both of these types of calculators and compare the results. Because of differences in the way programs are written, you're likely to get different results from each, even though you're entering the same information. Averaging the results of both programs will give you a rough idea of where your retirement plan stands.

Full Account

Don't get discouraged if the result of your retirement calculation is a huge number. Often the culprit is an unrealistic assumption that's inflating the number. If you've got sticker shock over the nest egg target you arrive at, it's time for a professional opinion. Online calculators produce estimates, and sometimes it is difficult to make the correct adjustments so that it matches what is likely to happen in real life. For example, I reviewed a retirement plan for a new client who was distraught over not being able to retire. She knew she couldn't retire, she told me, because an online calculator said she needed $200,000 more than she had. After talking a while, we realized that she would probably want to downsize her home when she got much older. Factoring in part of that future home equity put retiring soon within her reach.

Avoiding the Common Mistakes

The mathematics behind retirement calculations may give them the aura of a science, but retirement planning is unquestionably an art. The purpose of doing the calculations is to decide what you can do today to make your later years more financially secure. No matter what type of calculator you use, your results will be estimates, not bankable facts. Make your estimates as accurate as possible by avoiding these five basic planning errors.

Making Unreasonable Assumptions for Inflation

Assume 4 percent inflation when you do your calculations, but keep in mind that actual inflation may be much different. Inflation affects the cost of what you buy as well as the annual cost-of-living increases you'll see in your Social Security or pension check. Depending on what you buy, your expenses may increase faster than inflation. For example, regular household expenses may increase with inflation, but health-care costs may increase faster. If you have higher medical expenses than the average person, you may find your expenses will increase faster than theirs.

Rainy Days

Your company pension plan is only as strong as the company itself. If something happens to your company, the Pension Benefit Guaranty Corporation only guarantees basic pension benefits up to a monthly maximum that stays fixed based on when your company went bankrupt or closed the plan. Retiree health benefits are not guaranteed and can be dropped or changed by the company.

Allowing for increasing medical costs in retirement is difficult. One good way to account for this problem, if the calculator you're using allows it, is to assume smaller increases in Social Security and pension income than your estimate of expense inflation. If you assume 4 percent inflation, assume 2 percent annual growth in Social Security income. This change will put pressure on your nest egg to grow large enough to cover expenses later in retirement because your model Social Security and pension income won't quite keep up.

Projecting High Returns, Ignoring Investing Costs

Retirement calculators often suggest using historical economic returns for your portfolio. Making this assumption may cause you to underestimate the true amount of money you need. In fact, future returns may not be as high as past returns. Investment returns are linked to the inflation rate, so you'll be safer to assume a return no more than 3 or 4 percent greater than you use for inflation. If you assume inflation to be 4 percent, at most you should project for a portfolio return of 7 or 8 percent.

Investing costs can reduce your annual returns by 1 percent or more. These costs might be the annual expenses and sales charges in your mutual funds or the commissions paid on stock or other exchange transactions. The historical returns listed in retirement calculators are usually the returns of economic indexes like the S&P 500 or the MSCI EAFE Index, which aren't investments themselves and aren't affected by the costs your actual investments have. Check your total return assumptions against your actual portfolio performance—after accounting for expenses—to see whether your return projections are reasonable. If you're projecting a 7 or 8 percent return and want to account for investing costs, expect 6 or 7 percent returns.

Planning a Short Retirement

Even if you don't think you'll live to age 95 or 100, plan like you will. Planning for a long retirement is a good way to build a little extra into your target nest egg to make up for slower portfolio growth or higher inflation. You can see the effect of life span on the necessary size of your nest egg by running the calculator a few times using different ages. Adding five years makes a big difference. You can earmark this extra set-aside for medical expenses or long-term care expenses if you need them. If you try projecting to these older ages and your nest egg is coming up short, but you still feel you won't live that long, add an assumption into your plan for a part-time retirement job at the start of retirement or plan to sell your home and downsize at a very old age. Adding the home equity to your nest egg as you age may more accurately project what you may actually do and make your calculations more realistic.

Assuming Your Car Will Last 30 Years

Just because you're retired doesn't mean all those extra expenses you have now will stop happening. Leave room in your projected budget for big-ticket items that you'll still need to buy. If you're planning 30 years in retirement, you'll probably need to buy two, if not three, cars over the years. Your home will need maintenance and probably design updates. (You don't want to be the lady with the equivalent of the 1970s orange shag carpet in the living room, do you?) Medical emergencies and other unexpected expenses will still happen in retirement, just as they do now. When you input your projected annual—or monthly—income needs into the calculator, consider the average costs of these things into your budget. Don't assume that you'll be able to spend your entire monthly income each month and won't need to save for these nonmonthly items.

Planning to Pay Less Tax

The common assumption that taxes will be lower after retirement is based on the mistaken premise that, because you're not earning income, you'll pay less tax. This isn't likely to be the case. Many economists warn that tax rates will increase in coming years to cover the costs of the baby boom generation retiring with government benefits and to help pay down government debt, among other things. If your nest egg is invested in tax-deferred retirement plans, you'll owe income taxes on your withdrawals just as you do on your wages now. Run the calculators using the same tax rate you pay now to avoid underestimating the nest egg you'll need later on.

The Least You Need to Know

- Account aggregators like www.Yodlee.com can help you organize your accounts and track expenses.

- Monte Carlo simulation calculates the probability of an outcome and is an important part of a retirement calculator.

- Fee-only financial planners can help double-check the retirement projections you calculate for yourself.

- Tax rates are likely to be higher and investment performance could be lower in the future than over the past 40 years.

Chapter 6

Keep It Growing

In This Chapter

- ◆ Building a retirement nest egg no matter how tight your budget
- ◆ The power of compound interest
- ◆ Catching up if you're late to the savings game
- ◆ Account options when you change jobs

It's never too early or too late to start growing a retirement nest egg. And, most importantly, it doesn't require as much money as you might think. Whether you're new to retirement savings or have been growing accounts for years, this chapter helps you fine-tune your savings plan so it can thrive through job changes, child-care expenses, divorce, and virtually any other life challenge you'll face.

Setting Your Savings Target

Retirement plans have two basic characteristics—they act as a basket to help manage and organize your retirement savings, and they provide tax and employer incentives to help grow your nest egg. You should have two savings targets to match. The first job of your retirement plan helps make sure your savings meet your retirement goal, and the second helps you take advantage of money-saving and investment-boosting tax as well as employer benefits.

How Much to Save

Making regular savings a part of your everyday budget is a huge part of financial security, yet it is something almost everyone has struggled with at one time or another. The mantra "pay yourself first" is hard to follow when the bills are due and the paychecks don't quiet reach from payday to payday. If you're feeling stressed about accumulating regular savings for emergencies, let alone being able to save for retirement, and are sure you have no way to start, then start with these basic steps:

Nest Eggs

If you focus on saving and investing for retirement when you're young, you'll give yourself an advantage if you later want to reduce the pace during the high-cost childrearing years. Having a savings focus will also help you avoid building a lifestyle that takes your entire paycheck to maintain.

1. Make a list of all your expenses from the past month.

2. Divide the list into three categories: must have, like to have, and don't really need, and then total up each category.

3. Answer the question: what can I modify in the "don't really need" column so I can put that money toward savings?

These steps may appear pretty simple—and they are—but it's surprising how few people try this exercise on a regular basis. Little expenses can grow into big bills if you don't keep an eye on your total spending, and this exercise helps you identify places where you may have space to save. Run through these steps a couple times a year to keep yourself in check. Adding 1 percent to your savings account and 1 percent to your retirement fund will make a huge difference to you, both financially and in terms of an emotional sense of security and control. If you take money from something you don't really need, you won't even miss it.

There are many calculators online and in books to help you figure how much you should be targeting to save for retirement, and you'll find more details and calculators in Chapter 7. As a rule of thumb, though, you should target saving 15 percent of your gross pay toward retirement savings. This includes all the money you put into your personal IRAs or Roth IRA accounts, as well as your retirement plans at work and the amount your employer matches.

And while you're attending to your retirement savings, don't threaten that plan by not having emergency savings available. Set up a direct payroll deposit to savings of at least 2 percent of your gross pay. This will create a pool of cash to draw from for the unexpected, without having to deplete your retirement savings.

Getting the Match and Other Benefits

Your company match is a huge employee benefit. This is the amount your employer offers to contribute to your workplace retirement plan to match some of the money that you contribute. Your goal should be to deposit enough of your paycheck into your work retirement plan to at least earn the employer match. After all, it's free money!

Some employer retirement contributions take the form of matching your deposits, dollar-for-dollar, up to an amount equal to a certain percent of your pay, often 3 percent. Some employers put the bar a little higher and offer to match half of the first 6 percent that you contribute, up to a maximum of 3 percent of your pay. Be sure you understand how the match is calculated. In the first case, you'd only need to put in 3 percent to get the full match. In the second case, you'd need to contribute 6 percent of your pay to get their full 3 percent match.

Some employers make a profit-sharing contribution as a lump sum contribution to your retirement account at the end of the year. The term profit sharing sounds like an employer has to contribute to the plan only if he has a profit, but it really means that he's opted to decide on a year-by-year basis whether or not, and how much, he'll contribute.

Nest Eggs

Sometimes it can seem like the amount you're able to save or put toward a retirement plan is too small to make a difference, but every little bit helps and small amounts can accumulate fast. Think of it as "snowflaking" your account. Contributing small amounts very often, as in a winter snowstorm, can accumulate into something huge.

Profit sharing isn't directly related to how well the company is doing, but it's probably safe to assume that the employer won't spend the money to contribute to the plan if he's not doing well. Some companies make profit-sharing contributions even if the employee hasn't contributed to the plan himself, but he has to have at least opened an account. So check the plan document the company gives you each year, and ask questions to be sure your account is set up correctly to qualify for this retirement assist.

Pay attention to the plan vesting schedule, as well. The vesting schedule dictates when the money your employer contributes becomes fully yours, even to take with you if you leave the company. If you're planning on changing jobs, a quick double-check of when your employer's match will be vested may help you better plan your departure.

It's Never Too Early to Start

You can't start saving for retirement too early. As soon as you have income from work, open a retirement plan and make a deposit. As an example, one of the best gifts you can give your teen when she starts her first job is to open a Roth IRA for her. The money she deposits doesn't need to be the actual dollars she earns if her budget is maxed out paying for car, insurance, or other expenses. You can give her the money for the Roth IRA, up to the maximum for the year or her gross earnings, whichever is less.

Nest Eggs

As a rule of thumb, you may need a nest egg worth roughly 25 times your first-year expenses when you retire. If your expenses are $40,000 per year and you're expecting $10,000 per year from Social Security, you'll need $30,000 from your investments to make up the difference. This means you'll need roughly a $750,000 nest egg to retire.

Starting to save early for retirement captures the amazing power of compound interest and can make a small amount grow very quickly and very large. To see how this works, let's imagine that you deposited $2,000 in a Roth IRA account each year for 11 years starting when you were age 25 and ending when you were 35. A friend, the same age as you, decided to delay the start of her saving until she was age 35, then started depositing the same $2,000 per year and continued to invest that money for 21 years through age 55. You each earned 5 percent interest. When you both turn 55, despite having deposited only half what she did, your account is still larger than hers, thanks to compound interest. Following is how your accounts would turn out.

Power of Compound Interest at 5%

Age	Your Deposit	Her Deposit
25	$2,000	
26	$2,000	
27	$2,000	
28	$2,000	
29	$2,000	
30	$2,000	
31	$2,000	
32	$2,000	
33	$2,000	
34	$2,000	
35	$2,000	$2,000
36		$2,000
37		$2,000
38		$2,000
39		$2,000
40		$2,000
41		$2,000
42		$2,000
43		$2,000
44		$2,000
45		$2,000
46		$2,000
47		$2,000
48		$2,000
49		$2,000

continues

Power of Compound Interest at 5% (continued)

Age	Your Deposit	Her Deposit
50		$2,000
51		$2,000
52		$2,000
53		$2,000
54		$2,000
55		$2,000
Account value	$75,390	$71,439
Total deposited	$22,000	$42,000

Your friend deposited $42,000 but only had time to earn $29,439 in interest. Since you started earlier, you only had to deposit $22,000 to earn a whopping $53,390 in interest. Compounding really helped you.

The secret of compound interest is that each year's interest on your savings is added to the principal, thereby generating still more interest of its own. The cumulative effect is powerful.

Savings Tips for Young Families

Investing for retirement isn't always easy, especially when you have a young family and all the expenses that come with it. At this point in your life, being smart about how you balance your money priorities is more important than ever.

Downshift Your Savings During High Child-Care Years

Don't completely stop depositing to your retirement accounts when your kids are young and your expenses are high. After all, tax rules limit how much you can invest each year, and once the year is past, you can't go back and make up the deposits. If your budget is too stretched to cover child-care costs without running up credit card debt, try downshifting your savings to the minimum needed to collect your employer match. Be careful not to let the money you save as your kids get older and less expensive to care for creep back into your spending instead of your retirement accounts. As day-care and other costs decrease, allocate that money into your retirement accounts.

Don't Let Your Mortgage Eat Up Your Retirement

You'll be much less stressed about covering monthly expenses while also saving for retirement if you avoid spending more than 35 percent of your pay on your monthly home payments. If your rent or mortgage, real estate taxes, maintenance, and renovation set-asides account for more than one third of your gross salary, you'll feel the pinch. If costs are higher than 35 percent now and moving isn't an option, comb through your monthly expenses for places to save. Two of the best places to look for savings are the often surprisingly high costs of entertainment and dining out.

Enlist Your Family's Help

It's fun to buy gifts for children—so much fun that many families get carried away, and before they know it, their house is full of stuff, but their bank account is empty and their budget is crunched. Be candid with family and friends about gifts for you and your kids. It may seem awkward at first, but there's no reason to hold on to a tradition of excessive buying that isn't working. Most family members are anxious to help any way they can. If your extended family is spending money buying things you don't really need and, meanwhile, you are suffering from high expenses that are keeping you from saving, then no one is getting ahead. Instead, open a college savings account for family members to contribute to, or suggest gift cards for groceries or other items that will help you clear space in your budget for savings.

Full Account

I enjoy seeing people's reaction when I suggest that they revisit their holi-day gift-giving traditions and start talking to their families about money. It's especially fun in a group setting, such as a money management work-shop. First I get a lot of surprised looks, and then one or two brave souls will speak up in agreement. Before long, the whole room is abuzz with stories about peer pressure they feel around gift-giving and the true meaning of family events, in which gifts take a distant backseat to family togetherness. It's wild and exciting to see the consensus that generally forms around the notion that most people would rather reduce the gifts of "things" they get, in exchange for help building their nest eggs or their college funds. But it definitely can be hard—even scary or embarrassing—to be the first in your family to suggest to the rest of your family that gift-giving focus less on superfluous consumption and more on long-term finan-cial health. I suggest you take the first step; send a family e-mail suggesting a change, and then marvel at how many relatives agree with you!

Playing Catch-Up

While it's great to start saving early, it's never too late to start saving for retirement. If you're starting late, you may have no hope of catching up, but you'll be surprised at how fast the savings add up once you've got it on your radar screen.

First Step: Income and Expenses

Start by closely mapping out your current living expenses. If you don't have an expense-tracking system or don't like the one you're using, set up an online account aggregator mentioned in Chapter 5, like www. Yodlee.com or www.Mint.com, to help you. The aggregator will give you a quick picture of your overall expenses and make it easier to see what expenses you should change to make room in your budget for retirement investing. Many people are surprised to see exactly where their money goes each month and quickly see places they can make changes. Remember, every little bit counts; adding 1 or 2 percent of your pay to a retirement or savings account adds up quickly.

Once you have a good read on your monthly expenses, go through the spending list and check off those things that will change in retirement, such as commuting expenses, dry cleaning or uniform costs, and lunches at work. Next, add things to your list that you think will increase. This could include hobby expenses, travel, and additional health-care costs. Be as realistic as you can; try to imagine yourself retired today. What would you be doing, and what would you be spending? Sometimes people are discouraged from saving because they feel the goal is set too high to reach. They don't start because they're discouraged about their chances of succeeding. Creating a detailed retirement budget will help set your nest egg target at a reasonable level.

Nest Eggs

A fee-only financial planner can be a great resource to help you calculate the nest egg you need and the amount you should be saving. Fee-only planners charge only for their advice. They don't sell investment products for commission, and therefore have no conflict of interest in your investment choices.

Practice Retirement

A great way to find out if you can live on the income you're targeting your nest egg savings toward is to start practicing now. No, this doesn't mean you can quit your job and head for the beach! Practicing retirement means setting up your bank accounts so you can pay your work expenses from one and what will become your retirement expenses from another. Following the expense list you just created, assign one bank account to pay for the things that are exclusively work-related expenses and use the account you've assigned as your retirement bank account to cover everything else. Direct deposit your paycheck between the two accounts. With this system, you'll see pretty quickly what living on a retirement income amount will feel like. Plus, because you'll be closely watching your expenses, you may discover some places where you can shift money to savings.

Nest Eggs

Whether you have a partner or you're single, monthly money meetings (M&Ms) are an important part of keeping your retirement nest egg intact and your savings on track. Schedule 30 minutes a month to review your income, expenses, goals, and investments, and make adjustments as needed (see Chapter 1).

Transition Job

Planning for a retirement job is another way to boost your retirement plan if you've started saving late. A retirement job can be a toned-down version of your current job or something completely different. If you like what you do and it's something you can do part-time, great. If you're ready for a change, this is your chance to think outside the career box.

If your job involves lots of brain space and thought even when you're not at work, it might be fun to try something you won't take home with you. Would you like to work more—or less—with the public? Would you like to work outdoors instead of indoors or inside instead of outside? The beauty of a retirement job is that, because it's a supplemental income, you can worry less about trying something you may like only for a short time. You'll be able to try something fresh, and not necessarily long term, more easily than you were able to when your job was your living.

Once you've thought about your retirement job, find out how much you might earn at the job in today's market. Assume that the pay will increase in step with inflation and decide how many years you'll work. Then apply that purposed extra income to your calculation. You'll need less of a nest egg to retire if you're working part-time.

Back on Track After Divorce

Getting your retirement plan back up and running after a divorce can be frustrating. You may have had to divide your retirement accounts as part of the divorce agreement, and paying divorce expenses, such as lawyer fees, and supporting two separate households can wreak havoc on your finances. But don't let your emotions cloud your judgment about your retirement plan.

Avoid these three common planning mistakes:

1. Spending more than you can afford to maintain your old lifestyle. After your divorce, your income may not be enough to support what the two of you could afford when you were married, so be realistic about your resources. Review your income and expenses.

Keep your total housing costs under 35 percent of your income, and don't discount the idea of renting for a while, even if you owned a house when you were married. Recalculate your retirement savings target—or set your budget to deposit 15 percent of your income into retirement accounts until you have time to calculate a more definite target.

2. Using money to shelter the kids from the pain of the divorce. Divorce is painful for kids and adults alike, but don't get caught in a cycle of spending to try to make your kids feel better. Few families can break up and maintain the same lifestyle for each parent separately that the family enjoyed together. Don't threaten your retirement security by overspending on your kids.

3. Making your investments too aggressive to try to catch up or too conservative because you're worried about losing money. Don't throw your asset allocation out of whack because you're starting over with smaller retirement accounts and want to try to catch up quickly or because you're new to investing and are wary of risk and losing money. The asset allocation you pick depends on both your time until retirement and how long you'll live in retirement, as well as how you feel about risk. Go back through the exercise of calculating your asset allocation and make deliberate, thought-out changes to your new portfolio.

Full Account

I talk to a lot of people who have recently been divorced. Often, they're surprised and frustrated about the long-term financial results of their decisions. Sometimes they agree too quickly to get the divorce process behind them. Sometimes they prolong the process needlessly and end up with huge attorney fees. Divorce can be expensive, and you need good legal counsel. But don't be your own worst enemy by letting yourself get goaded into fighting for what you feel you deserve because you're emotionally hurt beyond what a court is likely to award you or that you really need. A good way to keep this clear is to do a rough financial plan early in the divorce process to get a general idea of what financial resources you'll need at the end of the process. When divorce settlements and negotiations start getting intense, refer to your long-term plan to remain focused.

Protect Your Nest Egg When You Change Jobs

Don't take the money out of your work retirement plan to pay expenses or bills when you leave your job. Keep it growing for your retirement by either leaving it in the employer's plan or moving it into your own IRA account. If your balance is greater than $5,000, most companies will let you leave your retirement account in their plan even after you stop working for them. After all, the plan sponsor—the investment company—would like to keep earning the fees they make on your account! Also, the government doesn't want to put a burden on you to move your account if it's not absolutely necessary; they want you to keep saving. You won't be allowed to contribute more to your old company plan, and your account vesting will freeze at the point that you left the company. But if you love the investments in your old employer's plan, if they are reasonably priced, and if there are enough choices to allow you to implement your asset allocation, avoid cracking your nest egg when you change jobs by leaving your account right where it is.

> **Rainy Days**
>
> If you take the money out of your employer's retirement plan when you leave, you'll pay income taxes on your withdrawal, plus a 10 percent penalty if you're under age 59½ unless you transfer it into another retirement plan. If you're in the 25 percent tax bracket, the extra penalty for not transferring to another plan could erase 35 percent of your withdrawal.

If you never liked your old employer's plan or if the plan has changed since you left the company, you can transfer your money into your Traditional IRA or a Rollover IRA account. The Rollover IRA works exactly the same as your Traditional IRA—with tax-deferred growth until you make a withdrawal, and withdrawals that are taxed when you take them, and required minimum withdrawals starting at age 70½. Use the Rollover IRA instead of adding your old work plan assets to your Traditional IRA if you think you'll want to transfer your work plan money into a future employer's plan. The Rollover IRA can work as a temporary holding account that will let you manage the investments until you have access to a plan to transfer it to. If you mix your work plan assets into your Traditional IRA, your new employer may not accept the transfer into their plan.

The Least You Need to Know

♦ It doesn't take much to grow your nest egg; a direct deposit of 2 percent of each paycheck into an emergency fund will grow faster than you think.

♦ You can have a retirement account as soon as you have income, or open a retirement account as a gift for your newly employed teen and help him fund it.

♦ Many employers will match your contributions to your retirement plan, up to a limit.

♦ It's okay to reduce savings when your kids are young and your budget is tight; just don't stop saving.

♦ You can transfer your balance from your old 401(k) to an IRA tax-free to continue growing your nest egg.

Chapter 7

Asset Allocation: Make Your Investments Work for You

In This Chapter

- ◆ Picking the best investment mix
- ◆ Getting the most for your money
- ◆ Special tricks for dealing with employer stock
- ◆ The benefits of a self-directed IRA

Ensuring you have the right mix of investments—a combination called your portfolio asset allocation—is an important part of protecting your retirement accounts. This asset allocation is a lot like a recipe for your portfolio. It tells you how much of each ingredient to add and helps you make changes to the recipe as you get older. But instead of flour, sugar, and baking soda, you're using stocks, bonds, and cash.

Picking investments without a recipe means you could end up with too much of one ingredient and too little of another. And this could mean your portfolio is too risky to let you sleep comfortably at night or not aggressive enough to grow into a nest egg large enough to meet your retirement needs.

Deciding on an asset allocation and sticking with it is relatively simple once you know a few simple skills. Online tools and special mutual funds, called target-date funds, make building and maintaining a healthy portfolio a piece of cake.

Getting the Numbers Right

Your asset allocation is a key part of building and protecting your retirement nest egg. The right mix of investments ensures you're being aggressive enough and taking enough risk to reach your goals, without making your accounts so risky and volatile that you dread opening your account statements each month, afraid to see a balance that might have taken another dip.

Full Account

When I first started my practice years ago, a new client came into my office with a perfect 50/50 portfolio; half her accounts were in stock index mutual funds and half were in bond index mutual funds, as they had always been. She had plenty of money to retire but still wanted my suggestion on how to rebalance. I showed her all the complex asset allocation calculations we financial planners make and described how she could completely optimize her portfolio to be the most efficient it could be. I produced reams of charts while she listened quietly. Then she asked a question that stopped me in my tracks: "Why?" She had saved enough to retire comfortably, and she lived beneath her means. What did it matter that her portfolio wasn't as optimally efficient as it could theoretically be? I think about that woman often when clients become bogged down trying to build the perfect portfolio, the portfolio that will beat their friend's investment performance. The point is to build a nest egg to achieve your life goals, not to wring every bit of return out of your investment as if it were some sort of competition. Focus on your goals and keep it simple.

Different Blends for Different Stages

You create this asset allocation recipe based on the eventual result you're looking for and your time frame, taking into account, for example, the size of the nest egg you need to build and how many years you have to do it. Then it's adjusted to suit the amount of risk you can emotionally tolerate. Two people who are the same age and have the same nest egg goal may have different asset allocation plans if one of them can sleep peacefully despite volatile dips and rises in his portfolio balance while the other prefers steady, predictable growth.

Your asset allocation plan will dictate how much of your portfolio you should put into each type of investment. This includes the three basic investment categories of stocks, bonds, and cash and also subcategories within each, such as *large-cap* stock and *intermediate-term* bonds. You might also decide to add alternative categories like real estate or commodities like gold and silver, adding a little more spice than the basic ingredients.

def•i•ni•tion

Large cap indicates the size, capitalization, of a company. The fuzzy dividing lines put large-cap companies higher than $5 billion, mid-cap companies at $1 billion to $5 billion, and small-caps below $1 billion. *Bond term* refers to how long a particular security takes to mature, from a year or less to 10 years or more. An **intermediate-term** bond is a bond that matures within the next 5 to 10 years.

The most common investment categories are:

- Large-cap U.S. stocks
- Mid-cap U.S. stocks
- Small-cap U.S. stocks
- Non-U.S. stocks from developed countries
- Non-U.S. stocks from emerging countries
- Short-term bonds
- Intermediate-term bonds
- Long-term bonds
- Cash

You should follow an asset allocation plan for three important reasons:

♦ You can better predict what the future performance of your portfolio may be by studying the historical performance of the mix you choose.

♦ It ensures that you own a variety of investment categories. Remember, the idea behind diversification is to reduce risk while maintaining or increasing expected returns—when one investment class is going down, others are hopefully increasing in value. Because you can't predict which class will do well at a certain time, diversification helps make sure you're always holding a winner.

♦ Asset allocation gives you a better chance to buy low and sell high. Part of following an allocation plan means you occasionally rebalance your portfolio back to the target mix. Taking cash from investments that have done well—selling high—gives you a chance to buy other investments at low prices.

Stocks are the most volatile of the three basic investment categories, but they've produced, over time, better growth than bonds or the most conservative investment, cash. This is why investors with long time horizons, like young investors saving for retirement, should allocate more money to stocks than to bonds and cash. The shorter your time horizon to withdrawal is, the fewer stocks you'll have in your mix.

Rainy Days

Asset allocation doesn't mean no loss. Many asset allocation tools will tell you how much—both up and down—the asset mix has fluctuated in the past. Convert the percentages they give you to dollars using the value of your portfolio, and test how you'd feel to see your account change that much.

You should choose the asset allocation based not only on your time horizon but also on how much volatility you can comfortably tolerate in your account. You may have picked the perfect mix for someone your age, but if the volatile swings in each monthly account statement discourage you from investing or, even worse, prompt you to sell all your stocks and just hold cash, then it's the wrong mix for you. If you're new to investing or not sure about your risk tolerance, try an asset allocation one level more conservative than your age bracket for starters. Once you're comfortable with the way your portfolio performs, you can readjust to the more age-appropriate mix.

Online asset allocation tools, like the ones at www.Dinkytown.com, can help illustrate varying allocations based on your time horizon to retirement and your concern about investment risk and volatility. You can also find online asset allocation tools at www.CalcXML.com and possibly your employer-sponsored plan's website.

Staying on Track When the Market Swoons

Different economic factors influence each investment class. In general, stocks do best during one part of the economic cycle, and bonds do better in another. This oversimplifies a very complex interrelationship, but it helps demonstrate why following an asset allocation plan works so well. Because each investment class takes its turn in the spotlight, each time you rebalance your portfolio, you'll be selling high and buying low. Here's why.

Initially, you'll start your asset allocation plan by deciding on your allocation and buying the investments in the percentages the allocation dictates. Let's assume you're a young investor with a long time before retirement, and you select 85 percent stocks and 15 percent bonds. Right away, market forces begin to exert their influence, and for the sake of discussion, let's say bonds are strong producers that year. After a year, you assess your portfolio and see that good bond returns and flat performance by your stocks have resulted in bonds now representing 20 percent of your portfolio. Rebalancing will mean you'll sell some of the strong bond instruments to shrink that over-weighted class, and buy stocks, which are comparatively cheaper in an economy that's currently favoring bonds. Rebalancing in this way, once a year, will help ensure you're buying the investments with the lowest prices and selling the investments that are higher priced. Rebalancing only once a year will also help minimize the trading costs—like commissions paid to your broker—that you'll have.

Nest Eggs

One of the advantages of rebalancing in a retirement account is that any taxes you might have owed after selling your investments are deferred.

Pie Chart World: Target-Date Funds

If annually rebalancing your accounts is something you'd rather not fret about, target-date mutual funds let you delegate this task to a professional manager. Target-date funds invest in a number of other mutual funds, following an asset allocation suitable for an investor with a particular time frame. They're named for the target retirement date that their asset allocation represents, so they're easy to spot. For example, a fund called Retirement Plan 2035 would have an allocation targeted toward investors retiring in 2035. As 2035 approaches, the fund managers adjust the asset allocation by reducing the stock and increasing the bonds and cash. By the time 2035 arrives, the mix of mutual funds in the account should be similar to the 50 percent stock and 50 percent bond and cash mix that's appropriate for a just-retired investor. Once 2035 has come and gone, the managers continue to reduce stock to create a more conservative portfolio over time.

> **Nest Eggs**
>
> Lifestyle funds are similar to target-date funds in that they are a mix of other mutual funds in an asset allocation that the mutual fund company chooses, but cater to risk tolerances. These funds usually carry names such as conservative investor or moderate investor and provide a fairly constant asset allocation based on risk tolerance.

You can use target-date funds and still tailor your portfolio a bit by choosing a fund that matches your risk tolerance instead of your target retirement date. If your expected retirement date is close to 2035 but you would like to be a bit more aggressive, you could use the 2030 fund. Conversely, if you want to be a bit more conservative, you could use the 2040 fund.

Target-date funds are popular choices in 401(k) and 403(b) plans because they take the guesswork out of picking investments and they're a strong option for employers to use as plan defaults under their auto-enrollment feature. The brochures showing the investment choices of these plans are full of pie charts showing the different asset allocations of each fund, creating what some employees call pie-chart world.

Just as individual mutual funds with the same objective, such as U.S. large-cap stocks, perform differently, individual target-date funds with the same objective perform differently as well. Your employer retirement plan will limit your choices to one fund family in most cases, but if you're investing in your personal account where you can pick the choices, compare the funds of several companies before deciding which one(s) to invest in.

Active vs. Passive Investing: Choosing Your Best Style

Pooled investments like mutual funds and *exchange-traded funds* (*ETFs*) are the easiest investments to maintain in retirement accounts because they're professionally managed and diversified. You're not left picking the individual stocks or bonds in the account; the professional managers do that for you. Investment funds follow one of two basic investing styles: active or passive. When you select investments to fulfill your target asset allocation, you'll need to decide whether you want actively managed or passively managed funds or a little bit of both in your accounts.

def•i•ni•tion

> **Exchange-traded funds (ETFs)** are pooled investment accounts like mutual funds in that they hold a basket of many individual investments. They are traded directly on the stock exchanges by investors buying and selling their shares like stocks.

Active management means the fund manager is choosing individual investments that her analysis shows should perform better than other similar investments. Active management costs a little more: the manager needs to be paid, trading costs occur when she buys and sells investments, and taxes are due on the investment sales.

Passive management follows the logic that it's unlikely that a fund manager will consistently beat the market over the long term, especially when factoring in the extra costs. Therefore, a passively managed investment seeks to simply match the market's performance. Passive investments are also called index investments because instead of actively picking investments, the management team simply buys investment instruments that comprise or replicate a particular market's index that they're meant to be tracking. Both index mutual funds and exchange-traded funds (also called index shares) follow this passive investment style.

You can build a good retirement portfolio using either actively managed mutual funds or passively managed index funds or ETFs. This list shows some of the funds that were recently in three popular target-date funds, as an example:

- ◆ Vanguard Target Retirement 2025 (all passively managed)
  Vanguard Total Stock Market Index Fund
  Vanguard Total Bond Market Index
  Vanguard European Stock Index
  Vanguard Pacific Stock Index Fund
  Vanguard Total Stock Market ETF

- ◆ T. Rowe Price Retirement 2025 (mixed passive and active funds)
  T. Rowe Price Value
  T. Rowe Price Equity Index 500
  T. Rowe Price New Income
  T. Rowe Price International Stock
  T. Rowe Price High-Yield

- ◆ Fidelity Freedom 2025 (mixed passive and active funds)
  Fidelity Disciplined Equity
  Fidelity 100 Index
  Fidelity Total Bond
  Fidelity Mid-Cap Stock
  Fidelity Diversified International

 Rainy Days

One negative of target-date funds is that they usually pull their investments from one fund family. Most families have specialties—Fidelity is known for their skill with stock funds, for example—so the target-date fund might contain some strong and some weaker mutual funds. If you were building your own portfolio, you could pick the best of the best and not be limited to one fund family.

If you check the makeup of these funds over time, you may find that the target-date managers have changed some of their choices. That's part of the beauty of a target-date fund—a manager keeps an eye on the investment choices in the account as well as the asset allocation. Notice that, except for passive management pioneer Vanguard, both

T. Rowe Price and Fidelity each use both active and passive funds in their accounts. Index maven Vanguard goes the extra step of including an ETF on its list.

On the Margins: Alternative Investments

Not all retirement plan investments are plain vanilla offerings such as stocks, bonds, and cash. Adding a small percentage of something a little more exciting like real estate or precious metals is a way to further diversify your portfolio. But the added risk makes it important to do quite a bit of homework before diving in.

Self-Directed IRAs

Self-directed IRAs are regular IRA accounts with all the same tax rules and characteristics that you've read about already. These special IRAs use the term "self-directed" to show that they are accounts that give you access to a broad list of alternative investments for your IRA. This can include any investment that is not prohibited by the tax law for IRAs. Common investments for self-directed plans are real estate and gold and silver. People who have self-directed IRAs are a sophisticated bunch, or at least one would hope they are. So the custodian of a self-directed IRA is much more passive than you'll see with a regular IRA account. They provide information about managing the account and often the infrastructure to deal with the unorthodox nature of the IRA investments. So it's very important to have good tax advice from a disinterested party like your own CPA or tax advisor if you decide to use a self-directed account, especially to avoid running afoul of the prohibited transactions rule.

Prohibited Transactions

Buying real estate or other fun investments like gold and silver might seem like a cool idea, especially if you have more money in your retirement account than you do in other accounts and you think you have an opportunity to make money in these investments. Unfortunately, contrary to what some self-directed IRA providers might imply in their advertising, you can't get any direct benefit or pleasure from owning these alternative investments in your retirement account. IRA investments must be true investments, not purchases of things that you want to use now. You can't live in the house your IRA buys, and you shouldn't count on jingling any Gold American Eagles in your safe deposit box.

A variety of prohibited transactions limit how you and your retirement account interact with each other. This includes all IRAs, but because the custodians of standard IRAs restrict you to a specific list of investments (the familiar stocks, bonds, mutual funds, and the like), self-directed plans are about the only place you might run afoul of these rules. The rules are:

- ◆ You can't buy property from your IRA or sell property to it.
- ◆ You can't use the account as security for a loan.
- ◆ You can't borrow from your IRA, and you can't lend money to it.
- ◆ You can't receive goods or services from your IRA, and you can't provide goods or services to it.

Real Estate—The Pitch

Real estate is an attractive investment to many people because houses and condos are much more familiar to them than intangible stocks, bonds, and mutual funds. One of the big pitches self-directed IRA providers make is to use a Real Estate IRA to buy your retirement home while you're still working. The idea is that, because of inflation, the vacation home will be more expensive in the future. Buying now will save money. Also, by renting the property to tenants until you retire, your IRA gains value from the investment. Once you retire and start using the home, your use of the property is taxable just like any other IRA distribution.

The difficulty with this scheme is that real estate can be costly to manage, and owning a single property doesn't give you any diversification. It's an alluring idea, but is it worth the risk of committing a prohibited transaction? For example, you can't provide services to your IRA, so something as simple as mowing the lawn at the rental property your IRA owns could be deemed a prohibited transaction. Once you break a prohibited transaction rule, your IRA gets treated as distributed and you owe taxes and penalties for that year if you're under age 59½.

It's easier to add real estate to your asset allocation by buying Real Estate Investment Trusts (REITs) in your IRA. You don't need a self-directed IRA to do this. REITs are basically mutual funds that buy properties instead of securities and are available from any brokerage firm just like other kinds of investments. This way you can enjoy the diversification of a real estate investment without the complexity and expense of owning real estate directly.

Gold in Your IRA

Investing in actual gold or silver in your IRA is easier than investing in real estate because you don't have the same maintenance problems for bullion or coins that you do with a home or condo. Easier doesn't mean foolproof, though. Be sure to use a self-directed IRA provided by a custodian that specializes in handling gold and silver. Custodians will often call these accounts Gold or Silver IRAs so they are easy to spot. The IRS says the gold needs to be stored in an approved depository, so you won't be able to enjoy displaying the coins or gold your IRA owns.

If you want to invest in gold without the hassle of owning the real thing, you can buy mutual funds that invest in mining company stocks or the mining company stocks themselves, in your regular IRA.

Allocate Around a "Bad" Account

One of the challenges of managing retirement accounts is that their special tax rules make them less flexible and harder to change than nonretirement accounts. Your plan at work is probably the least flexible of all, especially if it's provided by just one investment house with a limited array of investment options. Because deposits into retirement accounts are capped each year, it's doubly important to make sure the investments you're using are reasonably priced and are good choices considering your asset allocation target. Often, you'll need to make investment choices in the accounts you have the most control over—your personal IRAs and your nonretirement accounts—to make up for weaknesses in your work plan options.

For example, most 401(k) plans offer an S&P 500 index fund, which is most likely the lowest-cost investment option in the plan. You can use this fund in your company plan and then use your other investment accounts—where you have more options—to buy the other parts of your asset allocation, such as your small-cap funds, bonds, or international stock funds.

Hidden Fees, Fine Print

Using expensive investments is never a good idea, but it's even worse in your retirement plans. If you're spending your limited deposits on investment fees and paying expenses with assets that otherwise would be growing tax-deferred (or tax-free if in a Roth account), then you're wasting a finite opportunity to strengthen your retirement security.

Here are some warning signs and tips on dealing with high fees:

- Limit your exposure to marketing and sales fees as much as possible, and look for investments with low management fees. Check the investment prospectus for commissions or sales charges, as well as annual fees for management or marketing—called 12b-1 fees. Avoid investments with sales charges by buying commission-free no-load mutual funds. The funds don't charge a sales charge. Check with your employer to find out if the funds in your 401(k) are no-load or if the employer has negotiated to have the sales charges waived.

- If you'd like to buy ETFs in your IRA (which, because they trade like stocks, will cost a commission for each trade), work with a discount broker like Schwab Investments, Vanguard, or Fidelity to keep trading costs down. Use ETFs when your account is static—you're planning on making a minimum amount of trades to invest or rebalance your portfolio. Instead, if you're investing every month, select a no-load mutual fund that doesn't charge a fee for each transaction to avoid paying commissions on ETF trades.

Dealing with a Pricey Employer Plan

Most employers work hard to ensure the plans they offer their employees are reasonably priced. After all, most executives and managers are participating in the plans themselves. If your plan is expensive, either because it's small and only offers mutual funds with high sales loads or it's invested in a high-expense annuity, you should look at using your other investments to counterbalance the cost.

The advantages of your plan at work are the deposit minimums that are higher than you can make to your IRA and the possible employer match. Even if your work plan is expensive, it's probably still worth contributing enough to get the full match. If you are in the 33 or 35 percent federal income tax bracket or live in a state with a high income tax such as California, New York, or Washington, D.C., it may be worth it to deposit the maximum to your work plan even if the fees are higher than you'd like. If this is your case, work hard to compensate by minimizing expenses in your other accounts.

If you're not in a high tax bracket and you can't afford to put the maximum allowed into your employer plan, you should look at whether a less-expensive personal account is better for you. If the most you can invest is $5,000 or less, then investing enough at work to get the employer match and putting the rest into a Roth IRA or regular IRA with lower fees may work better for you.

Fixing the Annuity Mistake

Variable annuities are investment and insurance products that combine the characteristics of a mutual fund with a life insurance benefit. The life insurance characteristic of the annuity places it under a tax regulation that gives the account tax deferral just like an IRA. Unfortunately, if the annuity is owned within an IRA, you are paying extra for tax deferral of the annuity, which the IRA already provides—this is a clear waste of money.

The number of companies offering variable annuities exploded after the tax reform laws of 1986, when many more companies entered the market. Many of the annuities offered have very high mortality and investment expenses. If you find yourself locked into one of these contracts, there are a few tricks for getting your money out and into an IRA with more reasonable costs.

Annuities charge two types of fees: annual fees and sales charges. The annual fees are account fees and mortality charges (essentially a life insurance premium) that are calculated as a percentage of the value of the account. You won't see these fees on your account statement, but they're being collected nonetheless, and they hurt the performance of your investment. Check the prospectus to see how they work in your specific account.

Sales redemption charges are made on withdrawals and represent a percent of the amount withdrawn. Fortunately, the percent charged decreases over time and usually disappears altogether within eight or nine years. This information is in the prospectus, but it's also helpful to confirm the withdrawal fee details with a quick call to customer service at the insurance company who manages your annuity. The time clock on declining sales charges applies separately to each deposit you made into the annuity and runs on a contract year (which starts from the time the contract was issued), not a calendar year. If you made only one deposit, then you can calculate your sales charge using the prospectus schedule and the contract date. If you made subsequent deposits, double-check your charge with the company before making the withdrawal—and being surprised by the fee.

To escape high-cost annuities, your goal is to do a direct transfer from your IRA that holds the annuity into an IRA with lower-cost investments. Be sure your transfers are direct transfers, not 60-day rollovers—you can make only one 60-day rollover per year.

♦ Start your move by transferring the amount the annuity will let you withdraw per contract year without a charge. This is usually 10 percent of the account value.

♦ Repeat this annually until the sales charge on withdrawing the remaining balance in the account is low enough so that it equals the annual fee you'll pay to stay in the account. This will vary with different contracts, but those amounts usually equal out two years before the sales charges vanish altogether.

Managing Employer Stock

Many large, publicly traded employers match their employees' 401(k) plan contributions with employer stock. The hope behind this scheme is to motivate the employees with a more direct interest in the fortunes of the company. Unfortunately, it can sometimes result in having too much employer stock in your retirement plan. Some investment gurus say you should invest in what you know, and you probably know your employer's company very well, but being heavily invested in the company where you're also earning a paycheck is too risky for safe retirement investing. Because of this, most companies will let you sell company stock made as an employer match fairly soon after it's deposited. Sell the stock, and reallocate it into your other plan investments when you can. Try to keep your total company stock allocation exposure in your portfolio to 5 percent or less.

What looks like employer stock in your account could be shares, or it might be a mutual fund type account invested in employer stock or investment units that change value based on the stock performance. If your employer stock is really straight stock shares or can be converted to shares, a little-known tax provision lets you transfer the stock out of your 401(k) when you retire and only pay tax immediately on the original cost of the stock (see Chapter 11). If you're employer stock has grown in value over the years, this might be a good strategy.

The Least You Need to Know

- Not all people the same age with the same nest egg target will be comfortable with the same asset allocation.

- Target-date mutual funds do the asset allocation work for you.

- Self-directed IRAs are standard IRAs whose custodian allows you to hold alternative investments like real estate and gold in the account.

- High-cost annuities are a bad idea in retirement plans.

- You should never have more than 5 percent of your 401(k) invested in employer stock.

Chapter 8

Against All Enemies, Foreign and Domestic

In This Chapter

- ◆ Protecting your retirement nest egg from short-term financial pressures and big emergencies
- ◆ Keep your accounts growing as you move from job to job
- ◆ Calculating the true value of a pension in retirement
- ◆ Split assets in a divorce to minimize tax problems later

A large part of protecting your retirement accounts is being able to deal with the little emergencies, the small challenges, and the big disasters in life without having to take money out of your retirement accounts. Even if retirement is your primary financial goal, putting all your resources into your IRA and 401(k) is not the best way to reach that goal quickly. Keeping cash on hand and buying good health insurance and disability coverage helps protect against the unexpected.

Life challenges, such as changing jobs or getting a divorce, shouldn't break the bank, either. Tax rules let you move retirement money among accounts without having to pay taxes on the transfer. And with care, you can continue your retirement tax planning even if you change jobs or have to split assets with your spouse in a divorce.

Don't Be Your Nest Egg's Biggest Enemy: Plan for the Unexpected

Many of the biggest risks your retirement accounts face are unavoidable and often unforeseeable. Whether you're dealing with a big expense, such as a medical crisis or a prolonged disability that prevents you from saving, or smaller things, such as unexpected car or home repairs, building and maintaining an emergency fund is a key part of keeping your retirement nest egg intact.

Filling Your Rainy-Day Fund

It's easy to let the day-to-day bills and the things we need or merely want to buy right away take priority over building savings. We don't like thinking that bad things can happen, so it can be hard to admit that we might need cash for an emergency. But the fact is, liquid cash that you can access quickly is critically important to avoid building credit card debt or having to tap retirement funds when something bad happens.

Remember these points as you begin to build your emergency fund.

- Admit you're not invincible—things actually can happen to you that you won't expect.

- Give yourself a pay cut. No kidding. Many people adjust their spending based on what's in their checking account. If you work this way, try having 2 percent of your paycheck direct deposited into a savings account. Make your savings out-of-sight, out-of-mind, and you'll build an emergency fund before you know it.

- Keep an eye out for small windfalls and extras, like cash gifts from friends, bonuses at work, and even cash refunds when you return something you don't want to the store. A lot of the time, this money isn't part of your monthly budget, so take advantage of the extra cash and put it toward your emergency fund.

Financial planners suggest keeping enough cash in your emergency savings to cover expenses for three to six months. This time frame is a good rule of thumb because many people would need about that long to find a new job if they were laid off. Disability policies usually have a 90-day waiting period, so you would need savings to cover expenses until policy benefits started. What's more, basing your savings amount on your expenses makes the account size fit with your lifestyle. Think of it this way: the emergencies you face are affected by the cost of the things you buy; an emergency repair on a $40,000 car is going to cost much more than a repair on a $10,000 car.

Full Account

Growing your emergency fund is often more about psychology than about having the cash to save. Many people, who'd be hard-pressed to save, find it easy to let small monthly costs for things they want, and don't necessarily need, gradually add to their expenses. Think of *needs* as things that keep you safe, warm, healthy, and fed—in the short term and in the long term. Of course, *wants* are those things that might make life more fun. Upgraded cable TV is a want; emergency savings so you can pay the electric bill if you're laid off is a need. Spend on wants only after you've covered the needs.

If you find it tempting to let small monthly expenses leak into your budget rather than to add to your savings, the challenge is in your head, not your wallet. Next time you find yourself saying "it's only another $20 per month for this splurge," try adding that $20 to your savings instead of spending it. In time, your mindset will change, and your emergency fund will grow.

A credit line, like a home equity line or available credit on a credit card, isn't a long-term alternative to building savings, but having credit available can be a good short-term safeguard while you're building your emergency fund. Earmark the credit line for emergency purposes only; don't be tempted to use it for costs you can plan for, such as vacation or holiday expenses.

Protecting Your Nest Egg from Medical Expenses

Medical expenses are one of the biggest threats to your financial security. Health-care costs are high, and you're not always in the position to comparison shop when the need for care arises. Your emergency fund can help pay for the things your health insurance policy doesn't cover. Make sure your health insurance policy is complete enough to protect you from having to draw down your retirement funds to pay for medical care.

Many people have health insurance as an employee benefit. In this case, your employer has offered a limited choice of health plans to choose from. If you get a choice—or even if you don't—find out what your plan will pay for and what your total cost could be if you had a major illness. Check the following features of your policy:

◆ **Premium.** This is the amount you must pay each month in order to have coverage. If you leave your job, your employer will let you keep your coverage under a plan called COBRA (Consolidated Omnibus Budget Reconciliation Act). You keep the same policy, but the subsidy your employer may have been paying to keep the premium lower for employees isn't there any more. If you pay the full premium yourself, this could mean a higher premium when you're unemployed, so include enough money in your emergency fund to pay the full unsubsidized amount for six months.

◆ **Co-pay.** This is the amount you have to pay when you receive medical care. Co-pays are usually billed at the time of each eligible event, such as a visit to a doctor or the emergency room or when you fill a prescription. The co-pay can be different for different services. The co-pay for a doctor appointment is probably lower than a less-likely event such as an emergency room visit or being admitted to the hospital. Health plans with higher co-pays will carry a lower premium than similar plans with lower co-pays. If you decide to save money on the premium, it's important to have money in savings to cover higher co-pays if they arise.

◆ **Deductible.** The deductible is the amount you have to pay before the policy benefits kick in. For example, if your policy has a $500 deductible, you pay the first $500 for care, and then the insurance pays from there. You still have to pay co-pays even after reaching the deductible. If your spouse, partner, or kids are on your plan, you will probably have a deductible that applies to the whole family. Make sure you have the amount of the deductible saved in your emergency fund.

◆ **Maximum annual out-of-pocket expenses.** Because you're still paying co-pays for services even after meeting the policy deductible, most policies will specify an annual out-of-pocket maximum. This limits the amount you will have to pay under the policy each year. Premiums and some co-pays don't count toward the out-of-pocket maximum. A policy with a higher maximum will have a lower premium than a policy with a lower maximum. The maximum is a good guideline to check your emergency fund against. If you have three months of expenses in your emergency savings account plus your health insurance policy out-of-pocket maximum, then you're in good shape to avoid having to tap retirement plan funds in a medical emergency.

◆ **Lifetime maximum benefit.** This is the total amount the policy will pay for covered care, forever. Once you've used up this amount—unless you live in a state that requires insurance companies to cover everyone who applies and can get another policy—your coverage ends. Check out your state's official website for information on whether or not it compels companies to offer guaranteed issue policies that don't deny you if you have a pre-existing condition.

A company can afford to charge lower premiums if it has a low lifetime maximum benefit of $1 million or $2 million. But you'd be amazed to see how fast a million dollars in medical bills can rack up when you're dealing with cancer or some other major medical catastrophe. It's best to look for a policy that has an unlimited maximum benefit even if the monthly premium is higher because of it.

Nest Eggs

The financial security of your insurance company is important—what good does coverage with a low premium and rich promised benefits do if the company can't pay your claim? Ask the company for its ratings from Standard and Poor's or AM Best to make sure you're working with a company that has strong financial credentials. Check www.AMBest.com or www.StandardandPoors.com for the insurance company's rating and an explanation of what the rating means.

Forced Out: Long-Term Disability

A big part of building and protecting your retirement nest egg is investing money into it regularly. This can be hard to do if a long-term disability keeps you from working because you're eligible to contribute to an IRA or other retirement account only if you or your spouse has earned wages. But that's not the only problem if you're sick or hurt and can't work. Not having an emergency fund or disability insurance to help you cover living expenses while you're not working can put your retirement accounts in jeopardy.

Nest Eggs

If you're permanently disabled and can't work or earn money at all—in the IRS's words, "you can not do any substantial gainful activity"—then the withdrawals you make from your IRA before age 59½ won't carry the extra 10 percent penalty.

There are two types of disability insurance: short-term and long-term. Each pays a benefit equal to a percentage of your wages when you can't work because of illness or injury. Unlike the coverage under your employer's workers' compensation insurance, the injury doesn't have to be job-related for your disability insurance to start paying benefits. Short-term disability (STD) coverage usually starts after only a few days of disability and most often lasts from 9 to 52 weeks. Some policies require that you exhaust your accumulated sick days at work before benefits begin and don't pay a benefit if the injury is work-related and covered by workers' compensation insurance.

Long-term disability (LTD) benefits have a waiting period of 30 to 90 days and pay you for a longer period of time than short-term coverage does, usually 5 years or to age 65, whichever comes first. Your long-term disability coverage could also pay a partial benefit if you can work but at a lower salary than you were once earning.

Many employers provide one or both types of disability insurance as an employee benefit. You can buy either one on your own if they don't, but the cost of short-term disability can be prohibitively high. That's why it's a good idea—and smart money management—to save the premium by self-insuring and keeping your emergency fund full.

Nest Eggs

Pay the premium on your long-term disability insurance yourself if you're given the option. Disability benefits from a policy you paid for are not taxable as income, so you get to keep more to spend when you really need it. You'll owe taxes on your benefit if your employer paid the premiums.

Keep It Growing When You Change Jobs

Very few people stay in the same job for their entire work career anymore. This is actually part of the reason why plans like 401(k) and 403(b) are more popular than less-portable pension plans. When you change jobs, you'll almost always have the option of leaving your retirement plan in the previous employer's plan. If you like the investments there, you may decide that's a good idea—and certainly more convenient than having to deal with moving the assets to an IRA or your new employer's plan. But having multiple plans to keep track of is not the best option in the long run. Consolidating your accounts into your IRA or your new employer's plan will make it easier to manage your nest egg. As we've already told you, be careful moving your retirement plan; the penalties for making a mistake are pretty steep.

You can use a 60-day rollover or a direct trustee-to-trustee transfer to move money between any two retirement plans. This includes moving from one IRA to another or consolidating several IRAs into one account, as well as moving money from an employer plan to an IRA. If you move money from a regular IRA to a Roth IRA, you'll owe taxes on the money you transfer because Roth deposits must always be after-tax money.

Contact the current trustee to initiate a transfer between your accounts. If you're changing jobs, you'll be working with the human resources departments from both your old and new employer to make the transfer. Except in the case of some 403(b) plans, which can remain unchanged as you move from one employer to the next, your old employer will give you a packet that contains information about your retirement plan and your options when you leave the job. They'll let you know whether you can leave your account with them, and they'll remind you of the tax consequences of taking a distribution from your retirement account without transferring it to a new retirement account. (It may seem like information overload, but these disclosures are all required by the law.)

If you decide to move your old 401(k) to a new account, the old employer will need to know whom to send the money to. That's where human resources at your new job comes in. They'll have the information the old employer will need either to electronically transfer your money or to make out a check for the transfer. If you want to move to an IRA, the trustee or the investment company you're going to use will have that information.

If you're over age 70½ and you change jobs, your employer might take the required minimum distribution (RMD) from the account balance before it cuts you the check for a 60-day rollover or makes a direct transfer to the new custodian. This is helpful if you are retiring, but it is not helpful if you're going to continue working and are transferring the money to your new employer's plan. Talk to both companies' human resources departments in this case—from both the old and new employer—to coordinate the transfer without the RMD, so you can keep your whole balance growing.

60-Day Rollovers in Detail

Under a 60-day rollover, the current plan trustee will give you a check in your name for the amount you want to withdraw. Ask the trustee not to withhold taxes from the withdrawal. If he does, you'll need to make up that amount when you re-deposit the 60-day rollover withdrawal back into your IRA or 401(k) account. A 60-day rollover might be the fastest way to transfer money between accounts because you're not waiting for two bureaucratic financial institutions to make the transfer between them, but it's also the riskier way. If you miss the 60-day deadline or are not able to deposit

Rainy Days

You can do only one 60-day rollover of the same funds per year. Once you've moved an account, you can move it again through a direct trustee-to-trustee transfer but not another rollover. This prevents individuals from continuously withdrawing and using the same IRA money in multiple 60-day stints.

the amount that was withheld for taxes, you'll owe tax and a penalty (if you're under age 59½) on the amount not deposited.

Remember: Direct Transfers Are Best

The safest way to move money between retirement accounts is through a direct trustee-to-trustee transfer. The transfer may happen electronically between both trustees, or the trustee you're withdrawing from may cut a check made out to the second trustee on your behalf, for example, "Pay to the order of XYZ Mutual Fund company for the benefit of Jane Smith." Even though you get the job of receiving the check in the mail and forwarding it to the new trustee, because the check isn't in your name, taxes aren't withheld. The check will be for the full amount of the transfer.

Pay Attention to Rules and Paperwork

It's worth your time and effort to pay close attention to the paperwork involved in opening or moving money between retirement accounts. Making a mistake could mean that the account loses its special tax benefit characteristics. This would cause you to both realize taxable income from the account and lose the chance to have the money in the account continue to grow tax-deferred. If you over-contribute to an account or contribute to an account that you weren't eligible for—remember the income limitations for a Roth account, for example—you'll need to withdraw the excess contributions and then pay a penalty. In either case, it's best to pay attention to what you're signing and to carefully follow the rules of the accounts. Fortunately, there is an easy place to get this information.

Always go to the source for the most reliable information. For retirement accounts, that source is the IRS. Their website, www.irs.gov, is full of surprisingly easy-to-understand guidance on all things tax, including the rules around retirement accounts. It's alright to use an unofficial website or a book to guide you and make the information easier to understand, but books and websites can be wrong or outdated—the final, timely authority is the IRS. Retirement plans are explained in a variety of publications that are available online. The information you might need includes the following.

- Publication 560 Retirement Plans for Small Business

- Publication 571 Tax-Shelters Annuity Programs

- Publication 590 Individual Retirement Accounts

- Publication 4222 401(k) Plans for Small Businesses

- Publication 4224 Retirement Plans Corrective Programs

Remember, in the end, you're responsible for complying with all the rules that regulate your accounts. If you need help, your tax preparer, accountant, Certified Financial Planner™, or the IRS can give you guidance. For your work plans, your best resource will be the human resources department, the plan administrator, or the financial institution acting as trustee. Call the customer service number on your account statement to get in touch with them.

Managing Your Retirement Accounts Through Divorce

Divorce is expensive—not only emotionally but also financially. There are a lot of decisions to make and negotiations to complete. When it comes to protecting your retirement security, pay attention to three important things: dividing assets with retirement tax planning in mind, calculating the value of your pension plans, and using QUADRO transfers to defer taxes.

Rainy Days

Try to be logical about the way you divide assets in divorce. One of the biggest mistakes is overstretching your budget to stay in the family home. If it took two paychecks to pay the mortgage and maintain the house before the divorce, it will be difficult to keep things going and still save for retirement on one paycheck afterward.

Keep Your Tax Planning Options Open

The emotional stress of divorce can complicate negotiations around dividing assets. It's important to try to come away from the process with a balance of liquid assets, such as savings and investment accounts that are not in retirement plans—taxable accounts—and assets in retirement plans. Remember that having both to draw from in retirement will help with tax planning. The taxable accounts will give you access to lump sums of money so you can do things, like buy a car or make home repairs, without having to borrow money or make large taxable withdrawals from your retirement accounts. Try to work out the divorce settlement so you end up with your three money baskets: savings, taxable investments, and retirement accounts.

The best way to end up with a tax-smart balance is to list all the assets you are going to divide into three categories: savings and taxable investments, retirement accounts, and liquid assets such as houses or pensions. Then approximate the value of each, after-tax. When you negotiate, use the after-tax values as a guide to separating the assets fairly.

To estimate the after-tax value of each asset, calculate what you would be left with if you sold the asset and paid the taxes due.

- ♦ There's no tax on liquidating a savings account, so the after-tax value of that account will be the same as the current balance.

- ♦ Unless you have a lot of appreciated investments in your investment account that would incur capital gains taxes, the after-tax value of your taxable account would be the same as the current value.

- ♦ Figure the after-tax value of your retirement accounts by multiplying the total value by your marginal tax bracket and then subtracting that tax obligation from the balance of the account. For example, if your retirement accounts total $100,000 and your marginal tax bracket is 25 percent, the tax due if you withdrew all the money would be $25,000. Subtracting the tax from the balance of the account yields an after-tax value of $75,000.

- ♦ Initially, you can use an online resource like www.Zillow.com to give you an estimate of what your home is worth. For a more accurate number, you should have a formal appraisal prepared. The after-tax value of the home is the estimated value, less a realtor's fees, the cost of any major maintenance that would need to be done in order to sell it, and any capital gains taxes that would be due. If you're married or selling the home because of a divorce, you don't have to pay tax on up to $500,000 in capital gain. If you're lucky enough to have a home that has appreciated by more than $500,000 since you bought it, subtract the capital gains tax amount, 15 percent of the appreciation over $500,000, to arrive at the after-tax value.

Real Value of a Pension

Pensions are a little tougher to value than other assets with a fixed value because they offer an income for life. Be careful to figure a fair current value of a pension when you're looking at your assets.

Valuing the pension requires two steps. The first is to calculate the lump sum value at retirement age of all the income payments the pension is expected to make. The second is to calculate today's value of that future lump sum.

"Present value of an annuity" is the name given to the figure you're calculating in the first step. In this case, the word annuity means the stream of income payments and shouldn't be confused with the name of a product you can buy from an insurance company. The present value of an annuity figure is the nest egg you'd need to provide the same payments the pension promises. It's how much money you'd need invested in an account in order to receive regular payments equal to those the pension is going to pay.

For example, you have a pension that will pay $2,000 per month. The present value of that pension could be calculated as $420,000. This means that without the pension, you'd need $420,000 invested in an account in order to afford taking withdrawals of $2,000 per month.

A quick online search for "present value of annuity calculators" reveals a few easy-to-use calculators at websites like www.Money-Zine.com and www.Investopedia.com. The calculator will ask you for three numbers: the interest rate earned on the money per time period, the number of periods, and the payment amount. Make sure you keep your time periods consistent. If you're using the monthly payment, be sure to use the number of months and the interest rate earned per month. For example, to get the monthly interest rate, you need to divide the annual interest rate by 12.

To make the calculation, enter the earned interest rate that you would expect to make on your investment—say 4 or 5 percent—the number of time periods or the number of years you expect to live in retirement and receive the pension—30 years, for example—and the pension amount. The result of the calculation will be the value of the pension at retirement age.

Next, figure out how much you would need to have now in an investment in order to arrive at retirement with a nest egg the size of the pension present value. The calculator for this is called the present value. This calculation is easier if you do it in years, using annual interest rate as the rate per time period and number of years until retirement as the number of periods. If a pension's value at retirement is $420,000 and you have 20 years until you retire, using 4 percent as the interest rate means that the present value of the pension is $192,000.

Calculating the value of the pension this way will give you an idea of what this valuable asset is worth. Try the calculators a few times with different interest rates to see how using a rate a little higher or lower changes the numbers. Increasing the interest rate in either step reduces the value of the pension lump sum because higher interest means the same monthly payment can be received from a smaller lump sum of money. This calculation—and the interest rate used—could become a matter of negotiation. It's a good idea to ask your attorney or financial planner for help analyzing the pension value if you're not sure about your numbers.

QUADRO Is Your Friend

Fortunately, you won't need to take a distribution and pay income taxes on the amount you have to take out of your retirement account as part of the divorce. Using a transfer called a qualified domestic relations order (QUADRO), you can transfer all or part of your account to your ex-spouse's account without penalty or a tax liability.

QUADROs are a lot like retirement plan rollovers or direct transfers, except the transfer is between two different people's accounts. They require a court order, so they are a little more complex than regular transfers and often take longer for the plan trustees to complete. Some plans will also charge a fee for a QUADRO.

Rainy Days

Some government plans and plans not covered by ERISA rules may not allow QUADRO transfers. This is unusual, but double-check with your plan administrator before promising a QUADRO transfer in a divorce negotiation.

To minimize fees and to keep things as simple as possible, try to divide the assets with as few QUADRO transfers as possible. Instead of splitting all the retirement accounts 50-50, check back to the list you made of all the assets in after-tax value and plan a division that gives each party his share of the total assets while carefully keeping a balance of taxable and retirement accounts.

The Least You Need to Know

- ◆ An emergency fund equal to three to six months' living expenses is an important part of protecting your retirement from unexpected expenses.

- ◆ You don't have to leave your retirement account in a previous employer's plan; you can transfer to a new plan or your own IRA without paying taxes.

- ◆ The real value of a pension income in retirement is often more than you would expect and worth researching if you're divorcing a spouse who has a pension.

- ◆ A QUADRO transfer will let you move money between two divorcing spouses' retirement accounts without taxes being due.

9

When You Need to Dip Into Your Accounts

In This Chapter

- ◆ Where to get money other than your retirement accounts
- ◆ Which retirement plan withdrawals are exempt from extra penalties
- ◆ How 401(k) loans work
- ◆ What to do to rebuild your account after a setback

Unfortunately, despite careful planning, unexpected events can arise that require quick access to money. Once you've used up your other options to get cash—your emergency savings, credit card, or home equity line—you may be faced with the need to tap your 401(k), IRA, or other retirement accounts to tide you through a crisis. This chapter explains what you can do to find that temporary cash assist and how to get back on track quickly after the crisis has passed.

Last Resort: Other Cash Options Besides Retirement Savings

Some situations are obvious emergencies: uninsured medical bills from a sudden illness, an unexpected layoff without the cash to pay the mortgage, or damage to your home or car that insurance doesn't quite cover. If you suddenly find yourself facing something like one of these frightening scenarios without resources other than your retirement account assets to help you, you could be faced with having to take money out of your nest egg to get you through the crisis.

Many retirement accounts are eligible for hardship withdrawals. But in most cases, you'll pay income taxes and penalties on the amount you withdraw—not a good plan if your goal is to protect your retirement nest egg. As an alternative, some work plans will allow you to borrow money from your account. This reduces the tax hit and leaves a way for you to get the money back into the account, but there are costs and lost opportunities when you take a loan, even when it's from your own account.

 Rainy Days

If you need to take money from your retirement account more than once, it's time to review your finances and shore up your budget. A strong budget includes: monthly savings for small emergencies and regular nonmonthly expenses like holiday costs and quarterly bills; good insurance coverage; car maintenance; and housing expenses that are less than 35 percent of your pay.

Before you decide to borrow against or permanently withdraw money from your retirement plan, check to see whether or not you can get any money from places like these.

◆ Check with friends or family to see if they'd be willing to lend you the money you need. Why pay the bank the interest when you can keep it all in the family? Online services like www.VirginMoney.com make the documentation easy and can make your payments back to your family or friends automatic and electronic. You can even offer your car or other asset as collateral for the loan. The electronic payments and collateral will keep the relationship on a

business level instead of a personal one. If your family has investments or savings paying lower interest than what you're willing
and able to pay, this might be a good option for you and them.

◆ Consider selling something you have of value. Do you have jewelry,
collectibles, kid's toys or clothes they've outgrown, or china you
haven't used in ages? These are all things you can sell online, put
on consignment, or sell through a pawn shop to get cash.

◆ Review your permanent life insurance policy. Having cash value
to borrow against isn't a reason to buy permanent life insurance
coverage such as whole or universal life (term insurance is best for
most people), but if you happen to have one of these policies you
don't need, you might tap it for cash.

◆ Peer-to-peer, or P2P, lending is a new trend in which strangers
can lend money to one another. Check out www.Zopa.com or
www.Prosper.com to see if these might be good sources of cash.

Rainy Days

Avoid payday loans. If your situation is so tight that your only resource
is either a payday loan or a withdrawal from your retirement fund,
you're probably better off with the retirement fund withdrawal. Payday
loans have huge interest and fees, and you're just robbing Peter to pay
Paul. What will you live on next week?

Hardship Withdrawals from Your IRA-Based Account

The rules for a hardship withdrawal are different depending on whether
you want money from your IRA or your retirement plan at work. You
can withdraw money from your IRA anytime. After all, it's your account,
and you're managing it. In most cases, the IRA withdrawal will be taxable as income, but a few exceptions listed next will excuse you from the
additional 10 percent penalty if you're under the age of 59½. Remember
that your Roth account must be past its five-year anniversary in order
for the earnings to be available without penalty. Also, distributions of
after-tax money, such as from a Roth IRA or the amount you contributed to a nondeductible IRA, are also not taxable.

Total Disability

If you're permanently disabled and unable to work, you can withdraw money from your IRA or 401(k) without owing the 10 percent penalty, though you'll still be taxed on the withdrawal as income.

Medical Expenses

If you're unlucky enough to encounter very high medical bills and need to tap your IRA or 401(k) to help pay them, try to bunch them into one year if you can. Withdrawals to pay unreimbursed medical expenses—costs not covered by health insurance—are taxable, but you won't incur the 10 percent withdrawal penalty if costs are greater than 7.5 percent of your adjusted gross income that year.

And if you're out of work, you won't owe the 10 percent penalty on withdrawals from your IRA if you use the money to pay health insurance after you've been unemployed longer than 12 weeks.

Education

If you need to withdraw IRA funds to pay for higher education expenses, you won't owe the 10 percent withdrawal penalty. This option isn't available on 401(k) withdrawals; you can take the money if your employer allows it, but you'll owe a 10 percent penalty in addition to paying income tax on the amount you draw out.

Rainy Days

Be very careful if you need to take an early withdrawal from a SIMPLE IRA account. If you've been participating for less than two years, the penalty tax on your distribution is 25 percent instead of 10 percent.

Qualified expenses include tuition as well as fees, books, supplies, and equipment for you, your spouse, your children, or your grandchildren less the value of any scholarship, Pell grant, or employer-provided tuition assistance you've received.

Buying, Building, or Repairing Your Home

The first $10,000 distribution from your IRA or your 401(k) or 403(b) to buy, build, or rebuild a first home is exempt from the 10 percent early withdrawal penalty. Like the education benefit, this benefit applies to more than just you. The home exemption applies to a first home that you, your spouse, your children, your grandchildren, or your parents can own.

When the regulations refer to a first-time homeowner, it's not as cut-and-dried as it sounds. A first-time homeowner actually might have owned a home before; under these rules a first-time homeowner is someone who hasn't owned a home for the past two years.

Hardship Withdrawal from Your Plan at Work

The IRS gives employers guidelines on when they can allow hardship withdrawals from your 401(k), 403(b), or 457(b) plan, although they're not required to offer the option. The withdrawal must be for, as the IRS calls it, an immediate and heavy need, and the withdrawal must be the only way to cover that need. Your employer can define the emergency as affecting you, your family, or even important people that you're not technically related to like your partner or their children. They can put strict rules on access to hardship withdrawals and will probably require you take as much of a loan from the plan as you're eligible for before allowing any hardship withdrawal.

Check the plan document to see how your employer operates. You'll probably find that if you take a hardship withdrawal from your work plan, you'll be barred from contributing to the plan for at least six months after the distribution. You can't transfer the amount you withdraw for hardship into another retirement plan such as an IRA. In addition to withdrawals made under a QUADRO or through the "substantially equal payments over five years" scheme for early retirees (which we explore in detail in Chapter 11), your employer can include some of the same things that are allowed for a hardship withdrawal from an IRA, plus the following circumstances:

- Funeral expenses: 401(k) withdrawal is permitted to pay for burial or funeral expenses.
- Home foreclosure: 401(k) withdrawal is permitted to prevent eviction from your home or foreclosure.

Borrowing Your Own Money

Some employers, who may or may not allow hardship withdrawals, will let you borrow money from your plan at work. These loans have limitations, but because the amount you borrow can be replaced, taking a temporary loan may be a better idea than a hardship withdrawal.

Loans

Most plans will let you borrow up to half your account balance—only the vested part, of course—up to $50,000. Loans are usually paid back over five years, except if you're borrowing for a home, in which case the loan term might be longer. As with any other loan, you have to make regular payments and pay interest. Payments are withheld from your paycheck, so you need to be ready for the reduced take-home pay. The interest rate is set by the plan, but it's usually the prime rate, plus a percent or two. The interest goes back into your plan, less an amount the plan keeps to defray the cost of administering the loan.

> **Rainy Days**
>
> The interest you pay on your 401(k) loan is withheld from your paycheck after tax, but unlike other after-tax deposits to your plan, you don't get a tax break on this money when you withdraw it in retirement. Instead, you pay tax on it again—another good reason to avoid a loan if you can!

Loans are still better than outright withdrawals, but they do wreak some mischief on the potential investment success of your plan because the money you've borrowed for other expenses is money that's not growing toward your retirement nest egg goal. What makes the situation worse is that many plans will bar you from contributing new money, or in some cases will limit your contributions while you're repaying the loan. If this is the case, you lose the tax benefit and the dollar-cost averaging benefit of the plan, plus potentially any available employer match as well.

Loans are tax-free because you're borrowing from your retirement plan account. But if you leave your job—voluntarily or not—before the loan is repaid, you may need to make a lump-sum repayment in a relatively short period of time, or the loan would be deemed a taxable distribution and could also incur the 10 percent early withdrawal penalty. Plans differ on this detail, so be sure you understand your plan's policy when you take the loan.

401(k) loans don't require credit checks and have little paperwork. In most cases, you can get a loan fairly quickly by contacting your company human resources department. The HR department may have some financial planning hoops they want you to jump through before the load is issued—just to be sure you fully understand the process and don't have other resources to tap—so be sure to talk to them well in advance of needing a check.

You can only borrow from the 401(k) of your current employer. If you've left the company and rolled your 401(k) money into an IRA, you can't take a loan unless your current employer allows you to redeposit the money into their 401(k) plan.

401(k) Debit Cards

To ease the administrative costs of managing 401(k) loans, some employers have started issuing 401(k) debit cards. The debit card basically gives you access to your 401(k) plan balance as if it were a credit line. Unlike regular 401(k) loans that have payment schedules and payments withheld from your paycheck, 401(k) debit cards generate a bill you pay each month. The debit card bills keep coming until the loan is paid off, even if you leave the employer. Other than having the same drawbacks of missing out on the investment opportunities in the 401(k), one of the big risks with the 401(k) debit card is that if you miss a payment, the whole loan could go into default, becoming taxable immediately.

Rebuilding the Account

If you've had to borrow from your retirement account or, worse, take a hardship withdrawal, you need to focus on getting back on track as rapidly as possible. One of the biggest benefits of retirement plans is the ability to invest on a regular basis to take advantage of dollar-cost averaging and the tax-deferred—or with Roths, tax-free—growth.

Most plans will amortize your loans over a five-year term. Suppose you take a loan for $5,000. If the loan is 6 percent, the monthly payment will be just under $50 per paycheck if you're paid bi-weekly. By increasing the payment you make to $75 per paycheck, you'll cut the term down to three years and save about $600 in interest. While you are making the payments, the $75 per paycheck isn't coming home with you to be spent. Once the loan is paid off, play catch-up with your plan by continuing to put the $75 per paycheck into your plan after it is paid off, in addition to the regular amount you were saving.

Another good way to rebuild your account after paying off a loan or taking a hardship withdrawal is to become careful about your money management. Only a little bit of care—and maybe some tough changes—can ensure you don't have to take money out of your plan again. Use this checklist of things now, so you won't need to dip into your plan again later:

- Track your income and expenses carefully with an easy-to-use online system like www.Mint.com or software that lives on your computer like Quicken or MSMoney.

- Hold monthly money meetings with your partner or alone if you're single. Encourage money talk in your family. Too often, family members run into trouble they could have avoided if they had asked for help earlier.

Full Account

Your first monthly money meeting following a financial emergency so great that it forced you to withdraw money from your retirement nest egg to recover could be a tough one. Don't let blame or negative feelings block what regular M&Ms are meant to accomplish. Financial planning—and the communication and space you create in a monthly M&M—is the best way to achieve your goals and to make sure you have options when events push you temporarily off course.

Focus this next M&M on discussing how you feel—in nonblaming tones. Share your thoughts about the recent setback, and talk about your long-term goals. Schedule a follow-up M&M in a few days. Put off discussing detailed income and expense information until then. Your focus now should be on moving forward—the best first step to doing that is redefining and recommitting to your goals.

- Adjust your retirement plan contributions to be sure you can afford them. It's great to focus on contributing to your plan—especially to get the employer match—but if you're not also able to afford an emergency fund and nonmonthly expenses like insurance, gifts, holiday costs, and vacations, you might end up in dire straits again.

The Least You Need to Know

- Friends and family, or even complete strangers, might be a resource for cash through peer-to-peer lending sites online.

- Your retirement accounts should be the last place you look for money in an emergency.

- Your work plan may or may not allow loans or hardship withdrawals.

- A loan from your work plan might require quick repayment if you leave your job, even if you're laid off.

Part 3

Ready for Retirement

Are you getting ready to transition out of your career? Whether you're planning to retire young or wait until you're older and can start taking your Social Security benefits, there are a number of things to consider. Our focus here is to help you plan so you can save taxes both while you're working and after you retire and manage your investment mix as you get close to the big day.

Are you already retired? Then these chapters will help you adjust your asset allocation so you don't outlive your money and assist you in organizing your cash flow to reduce the stress of living on a fixed income.

"He's been carrying that ever since he marked one year to retirement."

Chapter

Ten Years Before You Retire

In This Chapter

◆ Building your nest egg in the critical 10 years before retirement

◆ Making sure your retirement income goal will be enough to keep you happy and doing the things you enjoy

◆ Changing your investment asset allocation to make a smart transition to retirement

◆ Deciding whether or not to convert some of your nest egg to a Roth IRA

◆ Protecting your nest egg from the taxman, now and in retirement

Middle age can be a time of extremes, both positive and negative. For many people, this is an energizing period; incomes have stabilized, the kids are out of the house (or at least getting close), and mature couples have figured out who they are and have a better idea of where they're going than when they were younger and starting their marriage and family. Many people welcome the feeling of hitting their stride that middle age brings.

But for other people, middle age can be a time of stress, when family transitions, job changes, and health challenges make the years leading to retirement tougher than when they were younger. Regardless of whether you're doing well and feeling enthusiastic about the future or coping with some personal strain, paying extra attention to your nest egg now will help make sure your retirement years are secure ones.

The 10 years preceding retirement is a crucial period that presents an important chance to focus on growing or catching up with your retirement nest egg savings. You need a plan to manage both investment risk and taxes now and after you retire. That means this is the time to check your asset allocation and the way you have your accounts organized among taxable and tax-deferred retirement accounts like IRAs and 401(k), and tax-free retirement accounts like Roth IRA and Roth 401(k) accounts.

Shifting Gears for Maximum Savings

Whether you've been building your retirement accounts for years or are just starting your nest egg from scratch, the 10-year point is a critical time for retirement success. Once you've done the retirement calculations described earlier and know how much you need to accumulate to reach your goals, it's time to scour the budget for money that's better spent on building your nest egg than on other expenses. Let's face it; if you're in your 50s, you've probably bought just about everything you need. If you haven't, you should have a pretty keen idea of the difference between what you actually need to purchase and what you'd describe as a luxury or nice to have. These three simple questions will help you clarify that distinction.

- ◆ Will I still own this and be actively using it in five years?

- ◆ Is this potential purchase something I decided for myself that I should have, not because of an enticing ad or because I want to keep up with a friend's lifestyle?

- ◆ Will this purchase help me reach my retirement goal?

If you're as focused on building
your nest egg as you need to be
in the 10 years before retiring,
you should be able to answer
"yes" to each of the three questions. You may find that just
taking the time to ask yourself
these questions—to deliberate
over your spending decisions—
will delay your purchase enough
that you'll find you really don't
need to buy it. Not surprisingly,
studies have shown that the more
advertising a person is exposed to, the more he tends to buy, despite the
fact that he might have no real or long-term need for the product or
service.

 Rainy Days

Americans feel a lot of
cultural pressure to spend
and appear affluent, especially when they're in their 50s
and older. Prove your financial
success by retiring earlier or
better than your peers instead
of being the one who has
the shiniest toys while he's
working but has to settle for
a financially shaky retirement.

Often, the process of deliberate spending is sabotaged by a compulsion
to "keep up with the Joneses"—a self-defeating determination to appear
as affluent as one's neighbors seem to be. This mindset, if you let it
control your spending behavior, can put your 401(k) and IRA retirement accounts at serious risk. Thoughtless or misguided spending will
leave you with less money to invest in your accounts. At the same time,
you'll be building habits and developing lifestyle expectations you won't
be able to maintain in retirement.

Finding Money in the Budget

M&M's—monthly money meetings—are especially important at this
age. If you're searching through the budget looking for ways to increase
your retirement savings, keeping a close tab on your expenses and
maintaining clear communication with your spouse or partner is very
important. Deciding to allocate more resources to retirement savings
than you have in the past will require changes to your lifestyle.
Whether you're single or in a household relationship, these changes
could add some tension to your life. Keeping the greater purpose for
the lifestyle change in mind by reviewing your goals, income, expenses,
and investment accounts in regular meetings will help reduce the stress
and increase the odds of success.

M&M's clearly make sense for couples in which one partner takes charge of managing the household money, but single people aren't off the hook. Planning regular time alone, focused on analyzing one's goals and money, will keep him on track, too.

Full Account

If money discussions, let alone organized monthly money meetings, haven't been part of your family dynamic, you may find the transition can be difficult. It's important to try, though, particularly as a way to help ease the emotional transition into retirement.

Money management while you're working is, in many ways, less complex than after you retire. While you're young, you have a thousand details of career and family to focus your attention on. It can feel a lot like plowing a field with your head down, simply pressing through the myriad of tasks. Going to work, building a career, raising your family, and getting through the day-to-day minutiae can easily fill your mind, giving you plenty to talk to your partner about.

Once you retire, many of the big life projects you've been absorbed in—career and family—are wrapped up. As you refocus your mind during retirement on the thing that's replaced your job as the provider of financial security—your nest egg—you may be surprised to find how differently you feel about your money. Regular money meetings, and perhaps eventually making money talk a habit, will help smooth the transition.

As you review your budget in your M&M, here are six key areas to find hidden money in your budget in order to increase your retirement savings:

◆ Prioritize the little things. Little expenses add up. Fortunately, small changes in your lifestyle add up, too. Be creative in finding and plugging money leaks. Don't go cold turkey; gradual changes are easier to stick with. Take your own coffee or lunch to work one day a week; get the car washed one less time a month; skip one manicure a month; hang a suit and wear it one more time before dry-cleaning it; rent a movie instead of going to the theater to see it. The ideas are endless. Decide now what kinds of small things you can change. Then set up an automatic direct transfer from your checking to your savings for the amount you'll save and watch it grow.

◆ Invest regular cost-of-living raises and bonuses. Many jobs include
regular cost-of-living (COLA) raises and some pay bonuses. Use
the COLA boost to increase your contributions to your work
retirement plan if you're not maxing it out already. Otherwise,
add the amount of your COLA to your traditional IRA or to your
Roth IRA. Use the Roth IRA if you're eligible, so you'll be building your after-tax/tax-free money basket for retirement.

◆ Invest the care-giving
partner's added income. If
one person stayed home
full-time or part-time to
raise the kids, you may have
an investing opportunity as
she creates or increases her
income as the kids grow.
Investing this new income,
while continuing to live
on the same paycheck you
raised your kids on, is a
great way for empty nesters
to turbocharge their savings.

> **Rainy Days**
>
> Many people count on
> an inheritance to fund
> their retirement. However,
> recent trends, such as elders
> living longer, higher-than-
> expected expenses for
> retirees, and greater ease in
> tapping home equity to cover
> daily expenses, will reduce
> what many will inherit from
> family. Planning on any inheri-
> tance is risky.

◆ Downsize the home. Moving out of the large home you raised
your kids in and into something smaller and less expensive is
the perfect way to free up money in your budget for investing. If
you're not planning to retire in the home you're living in now, a
break from the real estate taxes and maintenance costs can be a
welcome respite. And you don't have to buy your new place; tax
laws allow unmarried homeowners to realize $250,000 in capital
gains when they sell their primary residence without having to
reinvest in a new home. Married homeowners, or homeowners
selling because of divorce, get double the benefit, $500,000. If
you're planning to move to another location after retirement, take
the chance to rent now and learn more about your living prefer-
ences without having to recommit to the expense of owning,
especially if you plan to be in the home only a few years.

♦ Continue installment loan payments to savings. Are you finished paying off the car or home equity loan? Repurpose installment loan payments by investing them after the loans are paid off. If you were living fine while you were making the payments, there's no need to bring the extra income back into your budget. Invest it for retirement security.

♦ Put a stop to financially supporting adult children. One of the best things you can do for your children is to help them build their money self-esteem as early as possible. Take a close look at the money you give your kids. Once they're grown, it's time to stop the allowance and refocus those payments into your own retirement investing. It may be hard to say no to them now, especially if the amount you've given has been significant, but the best way to make both you and your kids more financially secure over the long term is to build your nest egg so you're not dependent on them when you're older. Stopping your adult children's allowance and your habit of picking up the tab for their expenses will also show them you have faith they can make it on their own.

Balancing Against College Costs

College expenses are one of the harder kid's expenses to balance against needing to save for your own retirement. A college education is an important part of financial success, and everyone wants what's best for their children. Nowadays, many career paths require a Master's degree or higher. This can put extra pressure on you and your kids to absorb education costs, so it's important to work together to plan how you will manage these costs.

Most people want a college degree to get a job that pays a higher salary. If this is the case, then college is an investment. But assess the return on this investment just as you would any other. Don't encourage your kids to spend more on school than they need to by offering to pay their tuition regardless of where they go. If you don't have savings already accumulated—savings separate from your retirement—to pay their college expenses, student loans for their education expenses are a perfectly appropriate option.

Your kids have their whole career ahead of them to pay back their loans; your resources need to go toward retirement, and with 10 years to go, you might not have time to pay off college loans and still save. Remember, you can't borrow money for retirement. If, once you retire, you find you have extra money, then perhaps you can help them with their loan payments, keeping in mind our advice in the previous section.

Keep It in Balance

This is an important time to keep an eye on your asset allocation. When you were younger, the long time that remained before you would start to make withdrawals worked in your favor. You could keep a higher percentage of your portfolio in higher-risk, higher-reward stock investments and take advantage of regular savings and dollar-cost averaging to ease the volatility of your account balances. Now that you're close to retirement, you may be more aware of your account balances and how much they change. You might even be tempted to move quickly to a more conservative asset allocation with more cash and bonds and with less stock.

On the other side of the coin, you might feel you're behind on your saving and be tempted to make your accounts more risky by adding stocks. Don't let your nervousness about nearing retirement deter you from looking at your asset allocation logically. You have a long-term time horizon as you'll probably live for at least another 20 years or more after you retire, so stocks should still be part of your portfolio. But don't overdo your allocation to stocks; your accounts need to be in the position to start making withdrawals soon, something you'll be loath to do if the market and your account balances are down.

Just as they're a good example of a diversified asset allocation, target-date mutual funds are a good example of how your portfolio's asset mix should change as you get closer to retirement. These funds adjust their asset allocation as appropriate for a moderate investor who plans to retire around a target year. For example, the T. Rowe Price Retirement 2010 manages an asset allocation for investors making the transition from career to retirement around that year. Recently, the asset allocation of the fund was 59 percent stocks and 41 bonds and cash. This compares to T. Rowe Price's asset allocation for people who have already retired as seen in their fund T. Rowe Price Retirement 2005,

Nest Eggs

Stocks are long-term investments that fluctuate in value over the short term. If this makes you anxious, hold more of your stock funds in a separate account and keep your more stable fixed-income investments in another. Think of the stock account as the money you're not spending for at least another 20 years, and the volatility might not bother you as much.

which recently had 50 percent in stocks and 50 percent in bonds. It's not a big change, but you can see that a fund serving those already in retirement holds less stock than the fund targeted to slightly younger investors. T. Rowe Price also has a fund called Retirement Income geared at investors who are even further into retirement and invested in an even more conservative allocation. The prospectus for this fund says that it will maintain about 41.5 percent in stock and the remaining percentage in fixed-income investments like bonds and money market.

The asset allocations that target-date funds use are good models of what you should be doing with your own asset allocation. Use an asset allocation tool like the ones found on www.DinkyTown.com or www.CalcXML.com to measure your risk and calculate your asset allocation more accurately. A good rule of thumb is to target a mix of about 60 percent stock and 40 percent in fixed income when you retire and then reduce the stock by 10 percent every five years until you have 15 to 20 percent in stock.

Rainy Days

It's important to have your radar up for unsavory sales practices when you're shopping for investments, especially at this point on your retirement timeline. Many companies target investors nearing retirement who are vulnerable and nervous about risk in their portfolios. Be especially wary of investments that promise stock market returns without stock market risk and investments offered as once-in-a-lifetime opportunities that can't be missed.

Taxes: Pay Now or Pay Later

A big part of protecting your 401(k) and IRA accounts takes place when you're nearing retirement—planning for taxes. Arranging the investments in your accounts to balance the tax benefits both now while you're working and after you retire is an important part of providing liquidity for nonmonthly expenses such as home repairs and car purchases, as well as making sure you don't pay more than your fair share of taxes on your regular monthly withdrawals.

Playing the Brackets

Income tax and capital gains tax rates are likely to be the same or higher in the future, so you need to use the years before you retire to make sure you'll have a tax-saving selection of options from which to draw income in retirement. Aim to arrive at retirement with as equal a balance as you can between the two basic types of accounts: tax-deferred retirement accounts and taxable or tax-free accounts. Tax-deferred retirement accounts, like your IRA and your 401(k), will cost you income taxes on the money you withdraw. Taxable accounts, like your regular mutual fund or brokerage account, and tax-free accounts, like your Roth IRA, give you access to withdrawals that cost you little or no extra tax when you are ready to tap them.

Capital gains rates are lower than income tax rates (and presumably still will be in the future), so start weighing your accounts so that the stock part of your asset allocation is more focused in your taxable investments accounts. Investments that are mostly taxed at income tax rates and offer lower capital gains, such as money market accounts and bond funds, should be concentrated in tax-sheltered retirement accounts like your 401(k) and Roth accounts.

For example, if you're shooting to retire with an asset allocation of 60 percent stocks and 40 percent bonds and cash, ideally you'd have most of your stocks in taxable accounts where you can take advantage of the lower capital gains tax rates when you realize gains from them. Fixed-income investments like bonds and cash would be held in retirement accounts. Retirement accounts shelter the income until you withdraw it and then tax it at regular income tax rates. If you're holding mostly stock in your retirement accounts, you're missing out on the advantage of being able to realize some income at the lower capital gains tax rate.

Follow these tips to make the adjustments you need in a tax-smart way.

◆ Pay attention to your tax bracket. One of the big advantages of investing in your 401(k), 403(b), or other employer plan is that your contribution reduces your taxable income. If your employer's plan has a good list of investment choices, you can build your bond allocation in tax-deferred accounts by contributing to the bond funds in the account. If the plan doesn't offer good bond funds, don't miss the opportunity for tax savings by stopping your contributions. Instead, contribute enough to the best stock funds available to qualify for the employer match (if any) and enough to keep your income below the top of the income tax bracket you're in. Review Chapter 3 for more information on how tax brackets work.

◆ Use your regular monthly investing to rebalance your accounts. Most people don't have enough money in both their tax-deferred retirement plans and their taxable investment accounts to simply swap where they hold the different types of investments. For example, suppose your goal was to have 60 percent invested in stocks and 40 percent invested in bonds. If your retirement accounts and your taxable investment accounts were equal in value, you could simply invest your taxable account 100 percent in stocks and your retirement plans in bonds and stock to meet the 60/40 asset allocation overall. Most people have more money in their retirement plans than they do in taxable investments, especially when they're 10 years away from retirement. Start to rebalance your accounts using your regular monthly investments. Buy the stock funds your asset allocation calls for in your taxable accounts and the fixed income in your retirement accounts.

The following tables show you how that would work. Suppose you have a $200,000 nest egg, divided equally between a retirement account and a taxable account and your target asset allocation is 60 percent stock and 40 percent bond.

Goal for the Whole Portfolio

Asset	Allocation	Dollars Invested
Stocks	60 percent	$120,000
Bonds	40 percent	$80,000

To meet the asset allocation, you need to have $120,000 invested in stocks and $80,000 invested in bonds. It makes better tax sense to keep the bonds in the retirement account and the stocks in your taxable account, so your separate account allocations will look like this:

Goal for the Taxable Account

Asset	Allocation	Dollars Invested
Stocks	100 percent	$100,000
Bonds	0 percent	$0

Goal for the Retirement Account

Asset	Allocation	Dollars Invested
Stocks	20 percent	$20,000
Bonds	80 percent	$80,000

Notice how each portfolio has a different asset allocation from the overall goal of 60 percent stocks and 40 percent bonds, but when added together they meet the target of having $120,000 invested in stocks and $80,000 in bonds.

To quickly implement this strategy into your retirement plan, you could rebalance your current account to 20 percent stocks and 80 percent bonds by buying and selling funds (or transferring between funds, depending on how your retirement plan provider works it) until you have the right mix. If you'd rather make the change more gradually—something you might do if the stock market is losing value while you're rebalancing—you could leave your current investments as they are but change how you direct new deposits. In this case, direct new deposits to 100 percent bonds. Check your asset allocation after a few months, and you'll probably see that it is getting close to the 20/80 mix in your retirement account that you're looking for.

Watch Out for the AMT

With all this attention being paid to what tax bracket you're in and whether you're investing in taxable or tax-deferred accounts, don't let the AMT, or *alternative minimum tax*, fall off your radar screen.

def·i·ni·tion

The **alternative minimum tax** was created in 1969 to close loopholes that enabled some super-rich taxpayers to pay no or unfairly low taxes thanks to legal tax shelters. It worked well when it was first implemented, but lack of inflation-linked adjustments has subjected a very large number of middle-class families to this tax.

For many people, the AMT is an extra tax they have to pay on top of their regular income tax. Unfortunately, AMT can affect just about anyone regardless of whether or not they have a high income. Among other things, if you have dependents for whom you claim exemptions, take the standard deduction instead of itemizing, pay state or local taxes, have high medical expenses, or pay interest on a second mortgage that you didn't use to buy or improve your home, you may find that you owe AMT. Check page 2 of your tax return Form 1040. A few lines down will be the line for AMT. If there's a number on the line, that's what you paid in AMT. IRS Form 6251, Alternative Minimum Tax—Individuals, details the AMT tax rules.

As you're planning your strategy to level your asset allocation between taxable and tax-deferred accounts, be very wary of AMT. If you paid AMT or if you have any of the factors that might trigger it, it may be important for you to continue sheltering your current income by putting as much as you can into your deductible employer plan. Talk to your tax preparer for help in making a tax projection based on different work plan contribution amounts. Or make a tax projection yourself using online tax planning software like that available at www. CompleteTax.com.

Are Annuities a Good Idea?

Annuities usually are not a smart idea at this point in the retirement nest egg game. Your target asset allocation should still have quite a bit of stock assigned to it. You shouldn't use an annuity to invest in the stock market, because you'll lose the tax advantage of being able to take capital gains from stocks sales at the lower tax rate. All the growth in an annuity is taxed as income when it's withdrawn.

You might understand the suggestion of investing in an annuity instead of a taxable investment account if you've maxed out the amount you can put in a tax-deductible plan at work and still need to put more away for retirement. But because annuities are tax-deferred investments, they wouldn't help you create the balance of taxable and tax-deferred accounts in retirement that you need.

Nest Eggs

If you're not sure you can live on the retirement income you're planning for, set up a test run by depositing an amount equal to your monthly retirement budget into an account, then use the account for the expenses you expect in retirement. This practice cash flow while you're working will help demonstrate what your retirement lifestyle will be like.

Converting to a Roth

If you're eligible, converting some of your IRA investments to a Roth account might be a good way of creating the balance of tax-deferred accounts and taxable or tax-free accounts mentioned earlier. Although you'll have to pay tax on the amount you convert, converting assets to a Roth could also help you save taxes when you reach age 70½ and have to start taking your required minimum distributions (RMD). Your RMD creates taxable income to you and is based on the total amount you have in regular IRA accounts. Roth IRAs don't count toward the calculation, so your RMD will be smaller. This could save tax because you won't be forced to withdraw the RMD income if you don't need to, and it will help you continue the tax-free growth in the account for later years.

Potential Tax Savings

Roth IRAs are relatively new, only about 10 years old, and you may not have a Roth account yourself yet. If most of your retirement assets are invested in regular IRAs and employer plans, such as 401(k)s and 403(b)s, your only choice for money in retirement will be to withdraw from these accounts and realize income tax on the amount you withdraw. You can start building money in a taxable investments account now to give yourself other options, but if you're eligible for a Roth IRA or a Roth conversion, you may do even better tax-wise.

You're eligible to convert some or all of your IRA assets to your Roth IRA in a year that your income (MAGI) is $100,000 or less. Use an online calculator, like the one at www.CalcTools.com, to help you calculate whether doing this will save you taxes in the long run. Consider these important facts:

◆ You'll owe taxes on the amount you convert.

◆ You need to have sufficient money, separate from the IRA dollars, to pay the taxes on the amount you covert.

◆ Keep an eye on your tax bracket when deciding how much to convert, because the amount you convert gets added to your other income and could bring you into a higher tax bracket. Roth conversions are not an all-or-nothing proposition. If you'll be eligible to convert next year, too, save tax by converting some this year and then some next year in order to stay in a lower tax bracket.

The online Roth conversion calculator will show you the growth of the account after conversion as well as the taxes due based on the income and growth rate you enter into the calculator. The income number you use for the year is your pay after deducting the amount you're contributing to your work plan. The calculator will ask you for a growth rate assumption to use for the investments in the account. Don't use a growth rate that assumes more than 6 percent.

Could Help Manage Minimum Withdrawals

A conversion now might be smart if you're lucky enough to have a pension or enough of a nest egg that you think you may not need all your IRA money in retirement and would like to minimize the amount you have to withdraw from the RMD to save taxes and to leave more to your spouse or kids. The advantage of the conversion increases the longer the money is in the Roth IRA, so making the conversion now is a good idea. When you make the calculation using the Roth conversion calculator to see if this is a good option for you, make the age you plan to take income from the account older than age 75. This will simulate the possibility that you don't take income until a later age, if at all.

Trend Watch: Retiring Later

Many people are continuing to work well into their 60s or even into their 70s. This seems like a good idea, considering that life expectancies are getting longer, too. Working, at least part-time, past the age when you can start drawing on Social Security is a good way to build on your financial security, not to mention keeping you socially engaged and challenged. Be careful, though, if you're planning to extend your work years as a substitute for putting sufficient money aside now for a financially secure retirement. Poor health could be a factor in your ability to continue to work. Plan conservatively by making your retirement projections so that your money will be enough if you need to retire in your 60s, take care of yourself, and don't assume—at least while doing your retirement plan projections—you'll still be able to work full-time past age 70.

The Least You Need to Know

♦ Your kids can borrow money for college, but you can't borrow money for retirement.

♦ To help save on taxes, organize your investments so that your taxable accounts carry more of your stock allocation and your retirement accounts hold your fixed-income investments.

♦ Annuities are a poor investment choice, partly because withdrawals are taxed as income and opportunity for income taxed at lower capital gains tax rates is lost.

♦ The way target-date funds change their asset allocations over time is a good model for how your mix of stocks and bonds should change as you near retirement.

♦ Plan your savings as if you plan to retire in your 60s, even if you think you'll work past age 70.

Chapter  11

Retiring Early

In This Chapter

- ◆ Taking income from retirement accounts and escaping the early-retirement penalty
- ◆ Managing asset allocation so you don't run out of money
- ◆ Picking an income option from your pension
- ◆ Planning for medical care in retirement using your IRA

It's a happy day when you do all the calculations and realize you can afford to retire early. Retiring completely to a life off the payroll or transitioning to a less-stressful, lower-paying job can be exciting.

However, planning to spend more years in retirement, supported by your nest egg, does take a little more planning. You need to take extra care to avoid costly mistakes and challenges that might drain your account faster than expected. So let's take a look at ways to continue to protect your nest egg against things like penalties, taxes, and medical care.

Minding the Special Withdrawal Rules

Retiring early means either that you'll depend on your nest egg longer than most folks because you're starting to draw from it at a younger age, or that you're planning to downshift your career to a point that you'll earn just enough to cover expenses without drawing from your nest egg, but you won't have the surplus cash to invest into it, either. No matter which flavor of early retirement you're planning for, it's still important to be extra careful to organize your accounts for income and convenience and to take advantage of special tax rules to save money.

Planning for Income

Money wasted on taxes is money you won't be able to spend in retirement. If you're planning to continue earning at least some income after you retire, you'll have the chance to continue organizing your nest egg accounts to give the most tax planning flexibility possible.

It's important to have three different sources of income or cash when you retire:

♦ Social Security and/or pension income.

♦ Tax-free or tax-managed income from accounts such as a Roth IRA, or the contributions you made to a nondeductible IRA, or regular taxable investment accounts in which you can pick tax-smart investments that are taxed at lower capital gains tax rates.

♦ Regular retirement accounts like IRAs and 401(k)s that are tax-deferred until you withdraw money and whose withdrawals are then taxed as income.

The purpose of the three baskets is to give you income tax–saving opportunities in retirement. Your first basket provides income that you don't have to manage: your pension or Social Security income. Think of your investment accounts—the part of your retirement income that you manage—as organized into the two remaining baskets based on the taxes you pay when you make withdrawals. The accounts in the tax-free or tax-managed basket, like your Roth IRA and the basis of your non-deductible IRA (the amount you deposited pre-tax), could be withdrawn without tax. Your individual or jointly held investment accounts can hold stock investments that are taxed at lower capital gains rates; these are your tax-managed accounts. The accounts in the tax-deferred basket, like your 401(k) or your IRA, cost you income taxes on withdrawals you take from them.

Nest Eggs

Remember that you can make penalty-free withdrawals from 401(k) accounts sooner than you can from IRAs. This is called making a separation from service withdrawal. If you're planning to retire no later than the year you turn 55, keeping your money in your last employer's 401(k) will give you access without the 10 percent early withdrawal penalty.

If your three baskets are not already balanced and you're still earning a paycheck, you have a choice of ways to fill the baskets that are short.

If your tax-deferred basket is short:

◆ You can add to an account directly from your pay by making contributions to your retirement plan at work or a deductible IRA.

◆ Instead of depositing money directly from your paycheck and reducing your take-home pay, you can still use your eligibility to make retirement plan contributions to shift assets from taxable accounts to retirement accounts. New contributions to retirement plans are based on the income you earn but don't necessarily need to be the actual dollars you were paid. If you need your whole paycheck for expenses but want to balance your investment baskets, you can fund your IRA contributions with money from your savings or other taxable investment account. If you want to maximize your retirement account at work, increase the amount you're depositing from your paycheck into your 401(k) or 401(b) and then use savings for monthly expenses if your lower take-home pay isn't enough.

If your taxable or tax-free account basket is short:

◆ You can add to an account directly from your pay by making deposits to your taxable accounts, Roth IRA, or nondeductible IRA.

◆ Convert part of your regular IRA to a Roth IRA. You pay tax on the amount you convert, but because you're retiring early, you're almost certain to reap the benefits of the tax-free long-term growth in the Roth. Check out the Roth conversion calculator at a site like www.CalcXML.com to see if it's worth it.

What's a 72(t)?

You can withdraw money from your IRA accounts anytime you want, although if you take cash before you turn age 59½, you pay an extra 10 percent penalty. If you have cash from other sources, like work or taxable accounts, tap these first, but if your IRA is the only option, a 72(t) can help.

Like so many of the strategies and accounts regulated by the IRS, the early IRA withdrawal strategy is named after the tax code paragraph that defines it. Paragraph 72(t) of the IRS code says that you can avoid the 10 percent penalty on your withdrawal as long as you make a series of substantially equal withdrawals at least annually. These substantially equal payments, or SEPPs, as they're called, must be calculated very carefully using one of three formulas: required minimum distribution, fixed amortization, or fixed annuitization. Each formula will give you a different allowed SEPP amount, so you can pick which method will work best for your circumstances.

Beware: the withdrawals you make must continue for at least five years or until you reach 59½, whichever happens *last*. If your SEPPs deplete the balance of the account before then, you'll owe the 10 percent early withdrawal penalty on the total of all of your 72(t) withdrawals.

The required minimum distribution is the easiest method, but it can result in the lowest SEPP amount. This method recalculates the withdrawal each year based on your life expectancy from the IRS chart and the balance of the IRA at the end of the previous year. This avoids depleting a small account, but the changing SEPPs from year to year can make budgeting harder.

The fixed amortization method and the very complex fixed annuitization method will usually give you a higher SEPP amount, but payments stay level regardless of what happens to the value of your account. This can be a problem if your account is small or if you leave it invested in risky investments.

There are a variety of online calculators to help you calculate your 72(t) SEPP plan, including tools on your investment account's site such as www.Fidelity.com or calculator sites like www.Dinkytown.com. As with all tax strategies, you're the one responsible if you calculate wrong; if you use a commercial calculator, note the careful disclaimer of responsibility they provide. That's a hint of how important it is to double-check your numbers with the IRS using Notice 89-25 from www.IRS.gov.

Company Stock in Your 401(k)

If you have your own company's stock, shares in your employer's company, not shares of a mutual fund that invests in it, you can transfer the shares out of your 401(k) after you leave the company and only pay income taxes on your basis, the amount you paid for the stock before it grew in value. This method is called net unrealized appreciation (NUA). When you eventually sell the stock, your profit will be taxed at the lower capital gains tax rate. Of course, this is only helpful if your company's stock is worth more when you decide to make the withdrawal than when you bought it. If the stock hasn't grown, there's no advantage to withdrawing it and paying income taxes on the amount. In that case, simply sell it in the 401(k) and then transfer the balance along with the other 401(k) assets to an IRA account in which you can pick the investments.

Some employers' company stock funds are convertible to company shares in order to take advantage of NUA. If your 401(k) has a company stock fund, you should check with the plan administrator or human resources to see if this option is available to you.

Nest Eggs

If you're planning to retire early, pay extra attention to diversification. Don't let the tax tail wag the investment dog. Many employers match employee 401(k) contributions with company stock. Even though there can be tax advantages to holding the stock until you retire, in most cases it's better to sell the stock when your company allows you to and buy something more diversified.

Planning Your Rollover

Most financial institutions such as banks, brokerage firms, and mutual funds give you a break in the fees they charge the more you invest with them. Organizing your investments into as few accounts as possible could save you account and investing fees. Having fewer accounts makes them easier to keep track of as well. A broker like Schwab Investments, Vanguard Investments, or Fidelity Investments can be a good place to consolidate your accounts because firms like these have an almost infinite number of investments available. They also have cash management services like checking and debit cards that give you convenient access to your investments and can make planning cash flow easier.

For example, if you're working at a retirement job, you can direct deposit your paycheck into your checking account and then easily make transfers into your investment accounts. Whether you're working or not, one way to make budgeting easier is to plan your income needs for the year and then set up automatic withdrawals from your investment accounts and retirement accounts into a checking account. This little trick will create a predictable stream of income that seems like you're still earning a regular paycheck. If your retirement job is sporadic, this will work especially well because you'll have a steady stream of income you can plan expenses around.

Asset Allocation for a Long Retirement

Unless you have a very large nest egg, if you're retiring young, you'll probably have more money in stocks than an older retiree with a shorter retirement time frame might have. Time horizon, and therefore the expected return on different types of investments over time, is more important than minimizing risk when you calculate your asset allocation. If you're retiring early, you have a longer time horizon, so you need more exposure to stocks in your accounts, and that means accepting a bit more risk to achieve longer-term growth.

Retiring at a younger age, though, doesn't mean that you're immune to the psychological effects of leaving your employment and the steady paycheck behind and moving into retirement. Retirees are often surprised to find that market fluctuations they once took in stride as workers seem more alarming to them now that they're relying on their nest eggs to provide income or to continue to grow without regular infusions of more savings. A review of the reasons that your asset allocation makes sense and a few tricks to level the inevitable ups and downs will help make early retirement money management less stressful.

Realize that your risk tolerance can change based on how you feel about the economy and that your partner's tolerance for risk could be much different than yours. As you're getting ready to retire early, pay extra attention to risk tolerance at your monthly money meetings. Each of you should complete a risk-tolerance questionnaire every three or four meetings.

You don't always have to use the same website risk-tolerance calculator. Mix it up. One quarter, pick the one from www.CalcXML.com; another time try the one on your broker's website or the one at www. AARP.org. Regular risk-tolerance checks will keep the noninvesting partner involved and give him a chance to discuss his feelings about your shared portfolio. This is often overlooked if one of you is assigned the job of managing the investments or meeting with the investment advisor. This extra step will also head off problems if the portfolio value changes more rapidly than the less-involved partner is expecting and will help him feel more comfortable with how the accounts are being managed.

Measuring your risk tolerance once a quarter will help you gauge how the economy might be affecting what you feel about investment risk. This exercise is meant to educate you about how your tolerance ebbs and flows with the economy and to keep you communicating about how you feel about risk. It isn't meant to make you change your asset allocation each quarter, especially since your age is a significant component in determining your asset allocation.

Changing the Mix

Factoring in your risk tolerance when you decide on an asset allocation is important. If the portfolio is too volatile, you'll have trouble sticking with the asset mix and might be tempted to sell investments when their value is down, which can do a lot of damage to your nest egg. In contrast, if the portfolio is too conservative and doesn't take enough risk, it may not keep up with inflation. The longer you need your nest egg to grow, the greater the risk of inflation cracking it. If you're planning to retire early, this means your asset allocation may have to be more risky and more volatile than you're immediately comfortable with.

Your age needs to be a bigger factor in creating your asset allocation than your risk tolerance, especially if you are retiring early and will need the nest egg to provide you income that keeps pace with inflation over your lifetime.

Let's try an experiment to see how this works. Pull out your favorite online asset allocator calculator. The one at www.Dinkytown.com in the "Investment Calculators" section works well for this comparison, so we're using the factors they look for in the following chart. Run two hypothetical scenarios: one for you, the early retiree, and one for your friend who is your age but plans to work to age 66. The assumption is that you and your friend both expect to live for a long time in retirement. The only difference between the two of you is that you're starting your retirement earlier than she is.

Input these assumptions so you can make an easy comparison:

Calculation 1: Your Early Retirement Plan

Age: 55

Current assets: $500,000

Savings per year: $0

Marginal tax rate: 25 percent

Nest egg income required: 3 percent

Risk tolerance: moderate

Economic outlook: moderate

Calculation 2: Your Friend's Regular Retirement Plan

Age: 55

Current assets: $250,000

Savings per year: $10,000

Marginal tax rate: 25 percent

Nest egg income required: 0 percent

Risk tolerance: moderate

Economic outlook: moderate

Notice that the only differences between the two calculations are the things that you would expect to be different between an early retiree and someone who is still in savings mode. The early retiree has a larger nest egg, isn't saving anymore, and needs income from her portfolio. The friend who's still working has a smaller portfolio, is still saving, and doesn't need income from the investments.

The result of this experiment shows you how important age is. According to the results of the www.Dinkytown.com asset allocator calculation, the assigned stock allocation for both you and your friend is within 5 percent of each other. She is still saving, and you're not, but because of your ages, your asset allocation is very similar. Retiring early means you'll have a more volatile portfolio, with more risky stock investments, than you would if you waited to retire when you are older.

Leveling the Bumps

One helpful way to smooth the upward and downward swings in your investment account balance as the economy vacillates is to segregate the more volatile stocks into an account that you can clearly, and psychologically, see as your long-term money. As short-term swings hit the account, you can take comfort knowing that its longer time horizon helps ensure that the underlying value trend is steadily upward. And, of course, that means you'll be keeping your less-volatile fixed-income securities, bonds, and cash in an account of their own. The steadiness of the fixed-income account will reassure you that you have cash and income available for current income needs even when the stock market is softening.

Let's look at a chart to see how this would work:

If you had a $750,000 portfolio with a target asset allocation of 60 percent stocks and 40 percent bonds, your goal for the whole portfolio might look like the following.

Goal for the Whole Portfolio

Asset	Allocation	Dollars Invested
U.S. Stocks		
U.S. Stocks, Large-Cap	15 percent	$112,500
U.S. Stocks, Mid-Cap	10 percent	$75,000
U.S. Stocks, Small-Cap	5 percent	$37,500
Non-U.S. Stocks		
Broad index	25 percent	$187,500
Emerging markets	5 percent	$37,500
Fixed Income		
Bonds	30 percent	$225,000
Cash	10 percent	$75,000
Total		**$750,000**

The most volatile asset classes would be small- and mid-cap U.S. stocks and emerging market stocks. These would account for 20 percent of the whole portfolio, or $150,000.

Volatile Asset Classes

Asset	Allocation	Dollars Invested
U.S. Stocks		
U.S. Stocks, Mid-Cap	10 percent	$75,000
U.S. Stocks, Small-Cap	5 percent	$37,500
Non-U.S. Stocks		
Emerging markets	5 percent	$37,500
Total	**20 percent**	**$150,000**

The less-volatile asset classes would be the large-cap U.S. stocks, the broad index non-U.S. stocks, and of course, the bonds and cash. These would account for 80 percent of the portfolio, or $600,000.

Less-Volatile Asset Classes

Asset	Allocation	Dollars Invested
U.S. Stocks		
U.S. Stocks, Large-Cap	15 percent	$112,500
Non-U.S. Stocks		
Broad index	25 percent	$187,500
Fixed income		
Bonds	30 percent	$225,000
Cash	10 percent	$75,000
Total		**$600,000**

The assets in the volatile asset class are meant to help your account grow with inflation. The money in this account has a much longer time frame than the accounts you'll start drawing on for retirement. By segregating the $150,000 in volatile assets into a taxable account, it will be easier to keep in mind that account balance fluctuations are an expected part of long-term investing.

Nest Eggs

Use a taxable account for as much of the more volatile assets as you can so you can take advantage of lower capital gains taxes on profits and be able to "harvest gains and/or losses" at year-end by selling investments that have lost money against investments with gains.

Pension Planning: Know the Numbers

When you retire early, you need to carefully compare your benefit options under your pension plan. Most pensions have four options:

 ◆ **Lump sum distribution.** This option allows you to receive a one-time lump sum distribution that you can roll over into an IRA and manage the way you take payments yourself. This benefit amount can often be too low to provide you with what you would receive through one of the other income options that follow, but can be a good option if you're concerned about the long-term ability of the company to make the pension payments or if you have a health issue that makes you less concerned with outliving your money and are more worried about leaving money to your heirs.

◆ **Option A, single-life annuity.** The single-life annuity pays the highest income amount but only pays during the lifetime of the pensioner. There is no benefit for the pensioner's widow.

◆ **Option B, annuity with one-third spousal benefit.** This option usually pays about two thirds of the full single-life benefit to the pensioner and then, after the pensioner's death, pays an amount equal to one third of the income to a widowed spouse.

◆ **Option C, which pays the same reduced payment for the life of the pensioner or the surviving spouse.** This option pays a 50/50 benefit. The monthly income amount is about half what it would be under the single-life option, but it remains the same after the pensioner's death for as long as the widowed spouse lives.

Other pensions may have more options, but they're always a variation on these basics.

In most cases, you can't change the option you choose once you start receiving a benefit. Some pensions, fortunately, will automatically reset to the full single-life annuity benefit if the spouse dies before the pensioner.

The lump-sum option often isn't available until you reach a typical retirement age such as 60 or 65, and in most cases it is substantially smaller than what you would be collecting through the regular income options A, B, or C. So if you're retiring early, you'll need to either wait for the lump sum to be available or pick one of the income options. Once you choose and start receiving payments, you can't change to another option. This is fine if you're single and just need to pick the single-life options, but it can be a problem if you're married and need to pick one of the lower-paying options with the spousal benefit.

Rainy Days

Most pensions require a spouse's signature if a married retiree opts for option A single-life or the lump-sum options because plan administrators are concerned that the spouse may not enjoy enough of the pension benefit if the pensioner dies.

The difference between the single-life income amount and the lower payments under option B or the still-lower paying option C is essentially like a life insurance policy on the person receiving the pension. The death benefit of the life insurance policy funds the spousal benefit part of the pension and pays the income to the spouse after the pensioner dies. Complications arise if you've chosen option B or option C and the spouse dies first. Because B and C pay less and benefits can't be changed once they're started, the pensioner is left at the lower pension amount, even though he no longer has a spouse to protect. This is like paying life insurance for no reason.

Some pensions solve this problem by automatically resetting to the full single-life benefit—option A—from option C if the spouse dies first. If your pension doesn't offer this reset benefit, use one of the calculators at www.Dinkytown. com to calculate whether or not it would be best to take the full single-life benefit and then use part of that additional income to buy a life insurance policy on yourself to benefit your spouse. If you die and your pension benefit stops, the policy would pay a death benefit, which your spouse could then use to replace the income loss of your pension. If your spouse dies first, then you can cancel the policy, and you'll still be at the higher single-life benefit.

> **Rainy Days**
>
> Not all pensions allow for unmarried partners to receive the "spousal" pension benefit. Take extra care to read the benefits description for the pension to be sure you understand who is covered and who isn't. If necessary, you may need to pick option A and then protect your beneficiary by buying a life insurance policy.

Medical IRA

Budgeting to pay for health care is important for any retiree but especially for people who retire before being eligible for Medicare at age 65. With luck and diligent care of your fitness throughout your working years, your need for medical care will be lower when you're a young retiree, but that doesn't keep you from having to pay the health insurance premiums.

One way to help is with a health savings account, also known as HSA or medical IRA. If you're interested in the details, check out IRS Notice 2008-59 at www.IRS.gov, but essentially an HSA is like an IRA in which you can deposit pre-tax money to pay for medical expenses. HSAs are just now becoming popular, and your employer may not offer HSA as an option at work yet. (Don't confuse HSAs with your employer's Flexible Spending Account or FSA.)

You're eligible to make deposits into your HSA if you have a high-deductible health insurance policy. Contributions are capped for each tax year, just like a regular IRA, but they are not taxable when you make withdrawals to pay for medical expenses. You have no minimum withdrawal requirements for the money in your HSA, so it can stay invested in the account until you need it, even past age 70½.

The Least You Need to Know

♦ Retirement accounts have special withdrawal rules that give access to your money before age 59½, but don't withdraw too much at once.

♦ You can withdraw company stock from your 401(k) and tax it as capital gains instead of income.

♦ Dividing your asset allocation across a couple of accounts—at least one for growth and one for income—will help you psychologically weather the ups and downs of holding stock in your portfolio.

♦ Most pension plans will reset to the top benefit amount if you outlive your spouse and you've chosen the spousal income option.

♦ Medical IRAs or health savings accounts let you accumulate an IRA-like account to help pay for medical care.

Chapter  12

Managing Your Plans During Retirement

In This Chapter

- ◆ Setting up your accounts to save taxes and make management easier
- ◆ Changes to make to your investment mix when you retire and as you get older
- ◆ Options for taking Social Security
- ◆ The alternatives to annuitizing a portion of your retirement account with an immediate annuity or managing the withdrawals yourself
- ◆ Asking for advice

Once you're retired, you need to pay just as much attention to cash flow, taxes, investment fees, and asset allocation as when you were working and building your accounts. Fortunately, today's online tools and web account access make managing and tracking your accounts easier than ever before. Access and organization aren't the whole story, though. Making sure you're living within your means can be tough in retirement because now you have to decide how much money to withdraw each month for expenses instead of simply managing your expenses within your take-home pay from your job. Setting up a regular monthly withdrawal from your retirement nest egg to your bank account will make it seem like the paycheck is still there.

While you were working, your employer had to be sure the company earned enough money to pay you your regular paycheck. Now that you're retired, a regular paycheck is up to you. This transfer of responsibility often makes retirees more anxious when they see swings in their retirement account balances. Balancing your income between steady, reliable sources, like Social Security or a pension and withdrawals from accounts invested according to a clear asset allocation that adjusts over time, is the best way to protect your 401(k), IRA, and other retirement accounts after you retire.

Organizing Your Accounts

In a way, you really can get away with less-than-perfect account organization and expense tracking when you're working because your regular paycheck acts as a sort of cap on your spending. Once you set up your paycheck contribution to your retirement plan at work and your direct deposit to savings or other spending accounts, you may not have had to think much about expenses or even taxes. Cash flow management is tougher in retirement because you need to plan withdrawals from an account that is bigger than your paycheck ever was. The large balance can seem enticing, and expenses can get out of control if you're not careful. But you can avoid this by setting up a retirement paycheck from your nest egg to your regular checking account. With a little planning, this will also help save taxes.

For Cash Flow

Here's how to organize your accounts for consistent cash flow:

1. Review your living expenses and decide how much income you need to cover regular monthly expenses like groceries, utilities, and mortgage or rent payments.

2. Calculate what your nonmonthly expenses will probably be. These expenses are things like quarterly real estate taxes, estimated tax payments, travel, holiday expenses, medical costs, and gifts. Then convert the total into a monthly amount.

3. The total of the monthly income need and the nonmonthly need must be less than you can afford based on your nest egg income and the income you generate from Social Security or your pension, because emergencies and surprising expenses will pop up in retirement just as when you were working. Keep these surprises from hurting your retirement accounts by making sure your planned-for expenses are below your means. This is the same principle as when you tried to live on less than your whole paycheck when you were working.

4. Assign a checking account, or a brokerage account with a checking option, that you'll use for the regular monthly expenses. You may find it easier to set up one checking account for fixed expenses such as car and insurance payments that can be made by auto-debit and one for the variable expenses like groceries and entertainment that are pay-as-you-go expenses.

The following example shows what the math might look like (notice for clarity, we've listed only a few of the possible expense categories):

Cash Flow Example

Expenses	Monthly	Annually
Step 1. Monthly fixed expenses		
Utilities	$100	
Groceries	$500	
Housing expenses	$1,500	
Personal expenses	$500	
Total	**$2,600**	**$31,200**
Step 2. Nonmonthly expenses		
Real estate taxes	$250	
Travel	$166	
Gifts	$83	

continues

Cash Flow Example (continued)

Expenses	Monthly	Annually
Holiday expenses	$83	
Medical expenses	$250	
Total	**$833**	**$10,000**
Step 3. Income		
Social Security	$1,700	$20,400
Amount to withdraw from nest egg	$1,733	$20,796
Total	**$3,433**	**$41,196**

Note: The total amount that could be withdrawn safely from the nest egg (according to a separate retirement calculation) is $2,500, which leaves $767 per month ($2,500 less $1,733) for savings.

Step 4. Set up an account with checking or online bill pay to receive the $1,700 from Social Security and $1,733 from investments each month.

Online money market accounts are a great way to organize these spending accounts. You can nickname them, as in our vacation example, so they're easy to track, and they earn enough interest to make sure you're not giving up too much growth on your savings by withdrawing it from your nest egg into an account that pays too little interest like a no- or very low-interest passbook or checking account.

To Save Taxes

Pay as few taxes as possible by reorganizing your accounts to be as tax-efficient as you can and then by making withdrawals from the accounts that are already generating taxable income.

Consolidate your work plans and IRA accounts into as few accounts as you can. A brokerage account will give you the most investment options. Then spread your asset allocation across both your retirement accounts and your taxable accounts so that more of the stocks are in the taxable accounts and more of the fixed income and cash are in the sheltered retirement accounts. Don't overdo it and leave yourself completely without cash in your taxable accounts, though; just as when you were working, it's wise to have three to six months of expenses set aside in a liquid account for emergencies.

The investments in your taxable brokerage account will naturally be creating some taxable income through dividends and/or interest whether you decide to make withdrawals from the account or not. You'll also generate capital gains from the mutual funds in the account from annual fund distributions or from selling investments to rebalance and keep your asset allocation on track. Because you're going to owe taxes on this money whether you use it as income or not, it's best to use this income in order to minimize the amount you have to withdraw from your retirement accounts to make ends meet.

> **Nest Eggs**
>
> Use a fully liquid passbook or savings account for the money you want to have quick access to. If you're holding a high balance, make sure you have FDIC coverage and are getting a good interest rate on the account. Stocks and stock mutual funds or ETFs are liquid, but you don't want to have to sell in a down market to deal with an unexpected expense.

At the start of each year, estimate what your taxable income from investments will be. Using your broker's cash management feature, set up an automatic withdrawal from your account so that you get a month's worth of this income paid directly into your checking account. Then set up a withdrawal from your retirement accounts so that the sum of your taxable withdrawal, plus Social Security, plus the retirement withdrawals, covers your monthly costs. In some cases, if the values in your accounts are not balanced between taxable and retirement, you may need to adjust which accounts you tap in order to manage taxes. Don't set up withdrawals that will deplete your taxable money faster than your retirement money or vice versa. It's important to keep the two as balanced as you can through retirement.

Adjusting Your Asset Allocation

Think of retirement as a transition for your investments, not a door you walk through into an entirely foreign financial landscape. You should do a few things with your asset allocation in addition to organizing your accounts for tax savings and cash flow, but most of asset allocation management in retirement comes down to dealing with inflation and making regular adjustments and reviews.

What to Do Right Away

Retiring is much like many of life's other transitions, such as getting married, starting a new job, and having your kids graduate from college. A good rule of thumb is to check in on your asset allocation calculations each time you go though a significant life transition. Retirement—whether you're still working part-time or not—undoubtedly counts as one of these transitions.

Full Account

M&Ms (monthly money meetings) are even more important once you retire. The process of regular meetings puts some structure around your money management, both your month-to-month planning and longer-term financial planning tasks such as asset allocation. If you are a couple, it will also keep the communication active, especially as you both transition into your new lifestyle. Hundreds of my clients have retired over the years, and it has been both a joy and a learning experience watching them move from earning money and investing to letting their money support them. But this transition can be more difficult than it sounds. It feels a lot different planning monthly withdrawals from your account than simply taking a paycheck and adding investments to the nest egg. Changes in account balance become a lot more important to you when you realize that the money needs to last you the rest of your life.

If you've been keeping your portfolio balanced following an asset allocation all along, you may find you don't need to make many changes as your portfolio is right on target. You might discover, though, now that you're retired, that your risk tolerance has changed a little. Find out how you feel about risk by completing a couple online risk-tolerance questionnaires at www.CalcXML.com or on your broker's website. Check your results against the asset allocation tools, rerun a retirement projection based on the new asset allocation (as a double-check that the asset allocation will be aggressive enough to cover your retirement income needs), and then compare the results to your current asset allocation.

Don't make any large changes in your portfolio allocation right away. Instead, if your new target is different from where your investments currently stand, change the investment in 5 to 10 percent increments over the next six months to a year to implement your adjustment.

Rainy Days

Account volatility can be unnerving, but inflation can have an even more insidious and corrosive effect on your retirement accounts. Unfortunately, you don't get monthly statements showing that effect—it's only noticeable over time. Rerun your retirement projections with your new asset allocation to be sure it's aggressive enough to keep pace with inflation.

Dealing with Inflation

A big reason behind keeping stocks in your retirement portfolio is to make sure your income keeps up with inflation. When you were working, you received regular cost-of-living or COLA increases. Now you have to give yourself regular COLA increases.

These three steps will help you deal with inflation:

1. Annually rerun your asset allocation calculator, which will suggest the amount of stock you need based on your age. Make the adjustments it suggests.

2. Track your expenses in an account aggregator, like www.Mint.com or www.Yodlee.com, so you can see how inflation is affecting you. The percentage your expenses have increased since last year amounts to your personal inflation rate.

3. Social Security income automatically increases each year in step with inflation. If you've planned your nest egg carefully, you'll be able to afford to increase your retirement plan withdrawals enough so that between the increase in Social Security and increase in withdrawals from your retirement accounts, you're covering your personal inflation rate. Rerun your retirement plan projections to make sure you can afford to increase your account withdrawals, and then make the adjustments to your direct deposits.

When to Review

Once a year, review your investment portfolio, asset location, and asset allocation; rerun your retirement projections; and reset your monthly income withdrawals. January is the perfect month because you'll be collecting information and documentation for your tax returns. The Social Security Administration will have reported their inflation increase in November, your Social Security check will have changed to its new monthly benefit amount, and you'll be receiving your year-end statements from your investment accounts by mail. Of course, this doesn't suggest you can ignore your finances through the rest of the year. Just as when you were working, continue your monthly money meetings (for more information on money meetings [M&Ms], see Chapter 1); check your accounts, income, and expenses; decide on any big or irregular expenses that might be coming up; and check on each family member's cash allowance amount.

Social Security Planning

Deciding when to take your Social Security benefit is an important part of protecting your retirement accounts and your long-term financial security. Taking the benefit too early—before you've earned your full benefit—could hurt your accounts as you're forced to withdraw from your IRA, 401(k), or other retirement assets to meet expenses. Withdrawing later might give you a higher Social Security benefit, but waiting might put pressure on your nest egg to cover current expenses.

You can draw reduced Social Security income benefits starting at age 62. If you were born before 1937, your full Social Security benefit was available when you turned 65. If you were born between 1938 and 1942, your full benefit is available at age 65 and some months. Folks born between 1943 and 1954 can take their full benefit at age 66. Right now, the age when you qualify for full benefits increases by a few months for each birth year until it reaches age 67 for everyone born in 1960 or afterward. If you work past your full retirement, your benefit will increase a little—partly because you're older and the benefit is calculated based on your shorter life expectancy but also because you're continuing to pay Social Security taxes that add credits to your account.

Every year, three months before your birthday, your Social Security benefit estimate statement should arrive in the mail. An estimate of your future benefit and the amount of Social Security taxes that have been credited to your account each year are included on the statement. Beware if you worked a job that wasn't covered by Social Security, because the pension from that job might reduce your Social Security benefit. Check out the Windfall Elimination Provision (WEP) or Government Pension Offset (GPO) calculators at www.SSA.gov to see how much.

If you decide to take your benefit before reaching full retirement age, there are limits to how much work income you can earn without a penalty. Currently there is a dollar "give back" for every $2 you earn over the earnings limit. If you're not working, drawing early can be an advantage even if it reduces your future monthly benefit because it reduces your need to withdraw money from other accounts to cover expenses. Use the break-even age calculator on the Social Security website to estimate the age you need to live to in order to benefit from waiting to draw on Social Security. If you think you'll live past the break-even age, it is probably better to wait until full retirement age to take your benefit.

> **Nest Eggs**
>
> Regardless of when you take your Social Security benefit, whether at age 62 or at a later age, you still must apply for Medicare health insurance at age 65.

If you're married, it's important to consider the effect on your survivor benefit of taking your Social Security benefit before your full retirement age. Widowed spouses receive their own Social Security benefit plus a part of their late spouse's benefit. If the higher earner is also the person with the shorter life expectancy—which is often the case of a husband with a wife a few years younger than him—delaying the higher earner's benefit will make the widow's benefit of the lower earner higher.

Check out www.socialsecurity.gov/estimator to calculate an estimate of your benefit. It takes roughly three months to process a Social Security income claim. You should contact the Social Security Administration either online at www.SSA.gov or in person at your local office three months before you want your benefit to start. The folks at the Social

Security office can be a great resource if you have questions about your retirement benefit or how any of the other benefits like widow's or disability benefit work.

When You're Single

If you're single, one of the bigger retirement concerns is making sure you don't outlive your money. Avoiding paying too much in taxes is a big part of preserving your money for as long as you need it. If you're not working, run the break-even calculator to estimate your break-even age—and decide from there when to start your benefit. If you're working, delay taking your benefit until full retirement age to avoid having your earned income counted against the benefit you receive. Once you reach full retirement age, it is usually better to start drawing your benefit unless your earned income is still more than you need to live on.

Nest Eggs

If you're divorced (and not currently married) but were married for 10 years or more, you're eligible for the higher of your own Social Security benefit or a benefit based on your ex-spouse's account. If you're divorcing someone who's paid more than you, it may be worth researching the financial impact of reaching the 10-year mark.

Right now, only up to 85 percent of your Social Security benefit is taxable as income. You should take the benefit if it reduces the amount of income you need from other 100 percent taxable sources you need, like retirement plan withdrawals. Don't take the benefit if it will only increase the taxes due on the income you already have coming in—such as from work—by bringing you up into the next-higher tax bracket. If you don't need it for living expenses, invest it and grow your nest egg.

If You're Married

For married couples, in addition to the tax considerations just described, the decision of when to take your benefit is complicated by making sure you keep the biggest survivor benefit. If you're married and are widowed, you can get a Social Security benefit that is about 50 percent of your spouse's benefit or the benefit you earned on your own account, whichever is higher. When your spouse dies, you can continue to receive your own benefit or a combined benefit that brings you up to the benefits the higher-earning spouse was getting. If you both worked and earned similar benefits, this won't affect you because you both are receiving your full benefit, on your own, regardless of the other spouse's earning history.

Complications arise if one of you didn't work or earned sufficiently less than the other. In many cases, this is the familiar scenario of the mom who stays home with the kids and the husband who spends more years in the workforce. For this stereotypical husband-and-wife team, it may be better for the husband to delay taking his benefit until full retirement age (or even age 70) in order to maximize the wife's survivor benefit.

 Rainy Days

If you're getting an early retirement pension from your employer, check to see whether your pension benefit includes a Social Security income offset. Your pension might adjust downward automatically when you turn 62 on the assumption that you'll start receiving Social Security then.

Annuitize or Not?

The word annuitize means that you take a lump sum of money—like that from a retirement plan—and convert it into a series of regular payments. Payments are usually timed to be monthly, but investors often choose quarterly or annual disbursements. A monthly payout is a good choice if you need monthly cash flow. Or pick quarterly or annual if you have a bill you need to pay on that schedule and want to use the annuity benefit to cover it.

The payments are structured to continue on a particular schedule that could be for your lifetime, for the combined lifetime of you and another person, or for a particular number of payments, say 10 years, for example. In the latter case, the annuity payments go to you or, if you die, your heirs, for a total of 10 years.

You can annuitize a sum of money by buying an immediate annuity from an insurance company. Alternatively, your retirement plan at work may offer an annuity option. If the work plan is a bona fide pension plan, you'll probably find that the lump-sum option is of much lower value than the pension's combined annuity payments over the beneficiaries' life span. Calculating the value is covered in Chapter 11. If your work plan is a regular 401(k) or 403(b) or if you're considering buying an immediate annuity with money from your taxable account or your IRA, it's important to stop and carefully do the math first.

Annuity payouts are usually offered as either a lifetime benefit or over a specified period of time. The best way to compare whether an immediate annuity is a good idea for you is to ask the insurance company for a chart outlining the income options you have. These are the standard options:

- Installment payments for a fixed period that pays a benefit for a certain number of payments, for example 5, 10, or 15 years, to you or your heir.

- Life annuity, which pays you for as long as you live.

- Life annuity with a guaranteed time period. Annuity payments would continue for your life or at least for a certain period of years.

- Life annuity with a refund, which would pay your estate a certain amount if you died before the annuity paid out the total amount you initially put in.

- Joint and survivor annuity, which pays you and a second person through the end of the longest of the two lifetimes. The income paid by this type of annuity is similar to the spousal benefit offered by regular pension plans.

Some annuities will offer variations on these payment options. It can be very appealing to transfer the responsibility of managing your money to the insurance company offering the annuity because the promise of regular payments for life almost seems too good to be true. Unfortunately, in many cases it is. If you calculate the present value (see Chapter 8) of the payments promised by the insurance company, you'll find that the amount the company holds back can be substantial. You need to decide whether this very large cut out of your nest egg is worth the comfort of regular payments.

If you decide you'd like to buy an annuity and invest part of your retirement nest egg, there are three things to consider when comparing companies and their annuity products:

1. Be sure the insurance company has high ratings from AM Best or Standard and Poor's. Go to www.AMBest.com or www. StandardandPoors.com to check the rating and to understand what the rating means. If you're relying on the insurance company to pay you a benefit over a long period of time, you want to be sure they are a financially secure company.

2. Keep the expenses in the annuity contract to a minimum by comparing the products from lower-cost companies like Fidelity, Vanguard, and Ameritas.

3. Don't buy if you don't understand the product or you feel pressured. Annuities are complex financial products. Give yourself the time to decide whether the product is right for you. If you're unsure, ask an advisor independent from the insurance company offering the annuity—like your attorney, accountant, or financial planner—for their advice.

Best Sources for Advice

Always get professional advice when you're deciding something as important as how to manage your finances in retirement, calculate an asset allocation, or buy an annuity. Fortunately, you have a variety of places to get good advice, unencumbered by conflicts of interest.

◆ Your company human resources department. If you're still working, you'll probably find that HR is full of programs to help you understand your pension or simply learn about retirement planning.

◆ Your accountant or your attorney. Many accountants and lawyers are experienced in helping people review their retirement options. Even if yours isn't, he probably knows someone who is. Check with your accountant or lawyer for a referral to a financial planner.

◆ Go right to the source. Organizations like the National Association of Professional Financial Advisors (www.NAPFA.org), the Financial Planning Association (www.FPAnet.org), and the Certified Financial Planner Board of Standards (www.CFP.net) offer searchable databases to help you find a financial planner near you.

Nest Eggs

NAPFA.org has a helpful questionnaire on its site with questions for interviewing prospective financial planners. Technical expertise is very important, of course, but so is making a personal connection with the planner. Make sure you're personally comfortable with the planner you choose.

Once you get a referral, you should expect a free initial consultation. This means that a prospective planner should be willing to sit with you for 30 minutes or so to discuss your questions and concerns and give whatever help you need from her. You might ask the planner to create a complex financial plan considering all aspects of your retirement plan and investments, or you might simply use her as a second opinion for the work and answers you have created for yourself. Either way, it's important to be actively engaged with your planner. Don't be afraid to ask questions, and be sure you understand what she is recommending to you before following her advice.

The Least You Need to Know

◆ When you retire, make changes to your asset allocation and investments over time—not quickly.

◆ Tax management in retirement is just as important, if not more important, than when you were working.

◆ Your government pension might reduce your Social Security benefit, so check SSA.gov for a calculator to show you by how much.

◆ Waiting to take Social Security until your full retirement age might be your best option, especially if your spouse earned less during his or her working years than you did.

◆ Most annuities have high fees, so do your research and check the present value of the benefits they offer before investing.

◆ Associations like NAPFA have online databases that you can search to find a financial planner to help you with your retirement planning.

Part 4

After You're Gone

If you plan it right, your retirement accounts will outlive you. These chapters are an important read for everyone, because here we explain how to organize your accounts so your heirs receive as much of your hard-earned nest egg as the rules allow. Don't ignore Part 4 if you're young and still working. Your accounts might still be small, but the needs of your family are probably pretty large at this phase in your life; these chapters will help you keep your family's legacy alive when you inherit a retirement account by carrying the value forward into your own secure retirement.

"No, boy! Don't do it! Leave it in the bank for just a few more years."

Chapter

Leaving It Behind

In This Chapter

◆ Balancing your kids' inheritance with your charitable inclinations

◆ Keeping taxes and medical costs from shrinking your estate

◆ Organizing your accounts and naming beneficiaries no matter what your age or stage in life

◆ Making changes when you remarry

These days, you don't have to be rich to have a high degree of potential tax liabilities, and you don't have to be a retired grandparent to be concerned about leaving your retirement accounts to your kids or grandkids. Retirement plans are a powerful way to build a nest egg, but many people don't pay close enough attention to what would happen to their accounts if they didn't live to use them completely and had to provide for passing their investments to younger generations.

Depending on how you have your finances and accounts arranged, the special tax benefits of your retirement accounts can be extended to your family. However, if you're not careful or if you're just unlucky, you may end up passing your account to someone you didn't intend to get it, such as a nursing home, or worse yet, Uncle Sam in the form of taxes.

No matter how you arrange your finances, we know the old adage is correct: you can't take it with you. Regardless of your age or how big or small your accounts are, it's important to manage your nest egg remembering you may leave it behind.

Charity and the Kids

One of the really amazing things about retirement accounts is that you can name any beneficiary you want for the account and that person or trust or organization gets the money after you pass, no matter what. Retirement accounts are not controlled by the probate process and your will. If properly managed, this can work great; if not, it can be a disaster. It largely depends on whether your beneficiary designations are up-to-date. The two most common places people want their money to go are, of course, to their kids and family or to a charity.

Balancing Interests

You need to put some deliberate thought into choosing the person or organization you write on the beneficiary form for your retirement accounts. Remember these basic facts about retirement accounts as you mull your decision:

- Everything you own when you die, including your IRA and 401(k) or its variant, is part of your estate, and, unless it's left to your spouse, could be taxed under the estate tax rules.

- The beneficiary has immediate and full access to your retirement account or part of the account that you leave to him. He doesn't have to wait to reach a certain age or meet any other requirement before accessing the money.

- If managed correctly, the beneficiary might be able to continue the tax benefits of keeping the money in the retirement account.

The first fact, that your retirement accounts are part of your estate and might be taxed, can be confusing. Right now the estate tax only affects about 2 percent of the people who die each year. In 2010, the federal estate tax is scheduled to be repealed, and then in 2011 it may be back, depending on what Congress decides to do about the tax laws. Your state may or may not have its own estate tax, too. (You can check with your state's department of revenue website to find out.) The important thing to remember when you're planning your estate and considering your retirement accounts is what the total of your other assets are and whether paying estate taxes will prevent your beneficiaries from getting the full benefit of inheriting your accounts.

Three good ways to protect your retirement accounts from estate taxes are:

◆ Leave them to your spouse because you can leave as much as you want to your spouse without it being taxable in your estate.

◆ Provide another asset, such as a life insurance policy, owned by a family member or a trust with you listed as the insured, so it doesn't compound the estate tax problem, to pay the tax.

◆ Leave part of your retirement account to a charity so that your estate can save taxes with the deduction.

It's important to review your estate's potential estate tax liability with your lawyer. Don't worry that the solution to save estate taxes will necessarily need to be an expensive one; it doesn't have to be. If you're young with a family, you should have enough inexpensive, term life insurance so your spouse or your children's guardian has enough cash to deal with any taxes without touching the retirement accounts. Your lawyer might suggest a trust to own the life insurance instead of you or your spouse to reduce the effect of the insurance on the estate tax. If you're older, you can leave a little money to charity directly in your will or through a trust to reduce the estate tax amount if your estate is taxable and you're concerned about the amount your kids get or the amount the government would tax.

Since the estate tax is related to how much money you have in your own name when you die, an inexpensive strategy your lawyer may suggest is to balance your total assets equally between you and your spouse by transferring nonretirement account assets between you. Remember, retirement accounts can't be shared, but as a married couple you can transfer nonretirement assets like brokerage or checking accounts or your home between you without paying tax. If one person has more in their retirement accounts than the other, lawyers will often have the spouse with the lower account balances own the house and most of the nonretirement accounts to make the value of what both spouses own equal. This can reduce the potential estate tax liability. Spouses in second marriages are sometimes uncomfortable with mixing accounts like this because under this plan the money they brought into the marriage could end up in their new spouse's account. Be sure you understand your lawyer's advice before making any changes to your accounts. Whatever they advise you to do, know that there are usually fairly inexpensive solutions to most estate tax problems.

Communication

Whatever you decide to do with your estate plan, you need to communicate your strategy to your family. If you're married, obviously your spouse will be in on your plans because you'll make them together, but many people neglect to tell their kids or other affected relatives what they have in mind. No, you don't need to go into every little detail with them. But check in on the basics, especially if your family is grown, because what you decide to do might affect their planning as well.

There may be details you don't want to get into now with your beneficiaries for various reasons, so leave that information in a letter. A simple letter, separate from your will so that it can remain private, is the perfect way to explain to your family what you had in mind when you set up your accounts and your estate the way you did, and it can avoid hurt feelings and family dissension later.

Stretch IRAs for the Kids

One of the really useful provisions of the tax law is that you can leave your IRA to your kids and they can take withdrawals over their lifetime. If your account is held with a trustee that allows it—most of them do nowadays, but it's worth double-checking the account agreement to make sure—your kids can inherit the IRA and then transfer the funds into an account that is still in your name but is now registered as a beneficiary account for their benefit. Minimum withdrawals are required, but they can be made over the child's longer life expectancy—extending the time the money stays tax-deferred.

A good way to avoid problems that can result when beneficiaries argue with each other about how to divide your bequest is to separate your IRA accounts so that each child is the beneficiary of an account. This is a little more work to manage, especially if it creates IRA accounts that are small and unwieldy to rebalance or that incur fees. If that's the case, this strategy may be practical only if you're retired and have a larger balance to work with. While you're young, you might just leave the kids as equal beneficiaries of the account and opt for easier management.

Beneficiaries can sometimes be mesmerized by the appeal of a bequest and start making lavish spending plans. If you're worried about your kids messing up the stretch IRA strategy by withdrawing more than the minimum required, or worse yet the whole balance, you can name a trust as the beneficiary. The trust must qualify as what's called a see-through trust. This means that, among other things, the beneficiaries are specifically named, and the trust becomes irrevocable upon your death, at which point the trustee can continue the stretch IRA for you. This would be a good strategy for a child who is permanently disabled, enabling the trustee to manage his disability benefits relative to the IRA withdrawals.

> **Rainy Days**
>
> If you're married, unless you're super-rich or have a lot of life insurance, your spouse probably needs to inherit your IRA in order to support herself in retirement. Don't automatically try to stretch your IRA to future generations and neglect to name your spouse as the primary beneficiary of your IRA if she needs the money.

The stretch IRA works for Roth IRAs, too, but doesn't work for many employer plans. Employers, or at least the trustees managing their plans, often don't want the hassle of managing beneficiary withdrawals over a long period of time. Their plan documents often dictate that distributions to heirs be made within five years. This is yet one more good reason to roll over your accounts to an IRA when you retire or leave a job.

Full Account
I'm being serious when I suggest you discuss the details of your estate plan with your kids. This is another area where financial planners have a perspective on people's finances that few others get a chance to see. Unless you ask them to, your financial planner won't discuss your finances with other members of your family.
However, we often witness the misunderstandings that can develop when families don't communicate about money. I've talked to parents who believe their grown children are financially independent and don't need a bequest, when the truth is far different. I've talked to kids who believe their parents are leaving them an inheritance, when in fact there is nothing to pass down.
Financial planners are skilled at bringing the parties together when they discover financially precarious misunderstandings like these. But why not work to bring your family together around finances and reap the rewards of being able to plan with the whole family in mind?

IRA Rollover for Charity

If you'd like to leave money to a charity, whether you're doing it as a tax break for your estate or from a moral commitment to a philanthropic cause, IRAs are good assets to give because the charity can receive them tax-free. Donating the IRA achieves your goal of supporting the charity, gets the estate the tax break, and leaves other assets you may have, like real estate or taxable investments, that would be less expensive for other family members to inherit.

If you're over age 70½ and are taking your required minimum distributions (RMD) from your IRA accounts, segregate the amount for the charity into a separate IRA from the amount you want to leave to a family member or friend. Beneficiaries have to continue the RMDs the original account holder started, based on the life expectancy of the oldest beneficiary. Charities don't have a life expectancy, so the IRS dictates that proceeds must be withdrawn fully within five years. Having a charity mixed in with the other heirs on the same account would limit the number of years the beneficiaries could stretch the IRA withdrawals to five years.

Naming Your Beneficiaries

Beneficiary designations are easy to make and easy to change. But don't let the simplicity fool you; pay careful attention to how you list the beneficiaries on your retirement accounts and review them each year when you go through the rest of your financial plan and investments.

You can make two types of beneficiary designations: primary and contingent. The contingent beneficiary only receives the account if the primary beneficiary dies before you do. Probably the most common beneficiary designations you'll see with couples is where the partner or spouse is named as the primary beneficiary and the kids or other family members are listed as equal contingent beneficiaries.

> **Nest Eggs**
>
> Always list both a primary and a contingent beneficiary unless you're naming something immortal—such as a trust or a charity—as a primary beneficiary. If you have no living beneficiaries, the proceeds of the retirement account go to your estate, where they must be liquidated and taxed.

You can designate multiple beneficiaries if you want—such as two of your siblings as equal primary beneficiaries and then a charity as a contingent beneficiary. In this case, both of your siblings would share the proceeds or, if one has died, the survivor would receive the whole share. If both your siblings were to die before you, the designated charity would receive the account.

If you have grandchildren, you may want the grandkids to inherit their parent's share of your IRA instead of the parent's other siblings, in the event the parent dies before you. In this case, list the parent as the beneficiary *per stirpes*. *Per stirpes* means that if the parent dies before you, their share goes to the deceased's siblings rather than being shared by your surviving children, who might have been designated as co-beneficiaries.

For example, if you named your three kids as equal beneficiaries per stirpes, and one of them dies before you, then their kids would be entitled to the deceased parent's share of the account. Without the per stirpes designation, your surviving two children would split the account and the grandchildren from the deceased sibling would get nothing. Most beneficiary forms give you the chance to check a box if you want to add the per stirpes designation.

Rainy Days

Don't list a person as a beneficiary if he can't use the money. This may sound counterintuitive, but inherited money in an IRA could reduce the benefits or access to services for someone on disability, for example. Listing a trust to benefit that person could be a better solution, but coordinate with the individual's legal advisors to be sure.

When you update your estate plan, your lawyer will make sure you have the right beneficiary designations and that all are worded correctly. The trustee of the account, the mutual fund company or brokerage firm that manages it, for example, will provide a form for you to list the name, date of birth, and Social Security number of each beneficiary. If you're naming a trust, you include the name of the trust, the date you are creating it, and its tax identification number.

If your instructions are longer than will fit on the form, most IRA accounts will let you file detailed beneficiary instructions in letter form. Work plans like 401(k)s and 403(b)s often don't have this flexibility, but always ask. They might not make it obvious when completing their form, but when asked, many can be quite accommodating—especially because they want to keep your account with them when you leave that employer.

Keep a copy of the beneficiary designation form or other paperwork that you used to name your beneficiaries. The trustee should send you written confirmation that any changes you make have been implemented. Many brokerage firms and mutual funds show your beneficiary designations online. In this case, keep a screen shot or printout with your other account statements.

Protecting Your Estate from Long-Term Care Expenses

Unless you have reliable retiree health care from your employer, the growing cost of medical care is probably on your fret list. Protecting your retirement accounts from the cost of long-term health care in a nursing home may or may not be completely possible, depending on the other assets you have, your age, and your marital status.

What's the Risk?

The thought of losing your hard-earned savings, not to mention carefully cultivated retirement accounts, to the high costs of a nursing home can be terrifying. Seemingly every day, we read about how much nursing homes can cost. And if you've ever visited a loved one in a nursing home, you're probably pretty sure you want to be able to afford the best one you can, should the time come.

But will that time come for you? The U.S. Department of Health and Human Services recently reported on the website www.Medicare.gov that by the time a person reaches age 65, there's a 40 percent chance he'll need to enter a nursing home. Health care is important, and high medical costs can do a lot of damage to one's financial security if he doesn't plan ahead. The trick is to use your head when you're planning and don't get carried away by emotion.

What's the Problem?

If you're young and working, you hopefully have sufficient health insurance to pay medical costs if you get sick or hurt and a disability insurance policy that you or your employer pays for that will protect some of your wages if your illness or injury keeps you out of work. And you have your youthful good health. Health is the key here because as long as the sickness is relatively short-lived or you recover from your injury, your insurance policies will keep your money and your retirement accounts safe. The problem arises when you don't get better or if your injury leads to a long period of decline or disability. That's when the insurance starts to fall short of the need. This circumstance becomes more likely the older or less healthy you are.

If you have assets or income and you want a product or service, you're naturally expected to pay for it. There are few other ways to acquire those things you'd like. Unfortunately, the huge potential cost of a long-term chronic illness is probably the one thing few of us have sufficient assets to pay for completely ourselves. The government recognizes this and provides two separate health-care programs to help: Medicare and Medicaid.

If you're over age 65, you have access to subsidized health insurance through Medicare. Medicare pays costs similar to what you expected from your health insurance provider when you were working. If you were sick or injured and needed medical treatment, your health insurance would pay for it—or at least pay toward it—and you would pay the difference through a co-pay or a co-insurance amount. Medicare health insurance works the same way. Very simply, if you need medical care, Medicare pays, within various policy limits and subject to deductibles.

Medicare doesn't pay much toward long-term care costs, though. Long-term care is health care to nurse a chronic condition that you wouldn't fully recover from and would need long-term health care to help maintain your quality of life at the highest level possible. This health care can be delivered in your home, at an assisted living facility, or in a nursing home. Unfortunately, prolonged care like this can be expensive. People are expected to use much of their savings or a retirement nest egg to pay for their own care. When their assets are depleted, they become eligible for care on the government's dime under the Medicaid program.

Protecting Your Nest Egg

You've worked hard to accumulate your retirement nest egg. One of the hopes is that your accounts will be large enough to keep your retirement comfortable in times of poor health as well as good. Protecting your nest egg so it lasts through a time of prolonged illness is an important part of that comfort.

If you're single, you might simply plan to use your assets to pay for your care when you need it. Assets can include your home—you might decide to sell your home and buy into a continuing care community, for example—and your retirement accounts.

If you're married, you don't have as much flexibility. Your spouse may want to continue living in your family home and may also need the income from your retirement accounts to live on. There are a few ways you can plan to help the ill person's spouse, often called the community spouse, maintain a comfortable standard of living should his partner need long-term care.

One way is to supplement your assets with the benefits of long-term care insurance (LTCI). LTCI pays a benefit if you need long-term medical care for a certain period of time. Like other policies, LTCI policies have waiting periods that serve a similar purpose to the deductible on your health insurance coverage, during which you'll need to pay for care before benefits start. Policies pay benefits usually in increments of a specified number of dollars per day, as either a flat rate per day or as a limit per day on expenses they will reimburse.

Higher-premium policies pay for a longer number of years and could even continue to pay for the rest of one's life. Because most people spend less than five years in a nursing home, many people who buy coverage save premiums by buying policies that pay for three or four years. Like your health insurance and your car insurance, you must pay most LTCI premiums forever, and you don't get anything back even if you don't use the coverage.

Medicaid eligibility is based on both your income and your assets. As an individual, you're expected to use most of your income and almost all of your assets toward your care. You can preserve your assets by giving them away before you need care, but that usually isn't the best option because, along with the assets, you give away your power to choose where you live and the level of care you receive.

Another option is placing your assets in an irrevocable trust, with a trustee to manage your accounts for you. This can be costly and complex, so it may not be the best choice when you're younger and just starting retirement. But as you get older and would prefer having a trustee to manage your affairs for you, a trust might be worth considering.

Ultimately, long-term care expenses are much like other expenses you have to plan for in retirement. For many people, earmarking the home equity or a retirement account that can be annuitized or liquidated to pay for care is the best option.

If you're married, the government realizes that it's harmful to impoverish the community spouse when this spouse needs long-term care, so certain assets are protected from the eligibility test you must pass to qualify for Medicaid. If you're worried about long-term care costs, these strategies might help protect some of the assets of the community spouse:

♦ Get married. Most protections, especially on jointly owned property, apply only to married individuals.

♦ Spend the older spouse's assets first. The community spouse usually gets to keep more assets than the institutionalized spouse. Spend the older, less-healthy spouse's retirement accounts first, and transfer the balances of nonretirement, taxable accounts to joint name or to the younger spouse.

♦ Pay off the mortgage and the car loan; the home and a car up to a certain value are usually considered assets. Pay off both using the income and assets of the older spouse so that the community spouse doesn't have to worry about these bills, especially on a limited income.

♦ Don't do anything, including buying LTC insurance and, especially before getting married or transferring any assets, without consulting an elder law attorney. Because Medicaid rules are always changing, this is an area where it is especially important to get good, current legal advice before taking action.

Decisions That Are Set in Stone

Fortunately, while you're living, you can't do much with your retirement accounts—other than electing to annuitize them and start receiving payments—that is set in stone. That changes when you die. At that point, a lot becomes set in stone, so review your accounts annually with these things in mind.

♦ Beneficiaries: Review these annually to keep them up-to-date and accurate. Don't rely on a beneficiary to be in a position to carry out your wishes other than to receive the account. If you're dead-set on a stretch IRA, then leave the account to a trust. If you want your heir to have the option of stretching the IRA withdrawals, leave the account to him or her directly. Use per stirpes designation if you want proceeds to stay divided between siblings' families, and don't leave your retirement account to one child with instructions to divide the proceeds between the remaining siblings as he sees fit.

◆ Beneficiary payout options offered by the account trustee: There is a lot of paperwork when you designate specific payout options for a retirement account. Don't forget to check, and annually review, to make sure the trustee will allow a stretched payout to the beneficiary.

Planning with Your Second Spouse in Mind

If you or your spouse has children from a previous marriage, take extra care to make sure everyone is considered if you die first. Communication is probably one of the more important things you can do, because whatever you decide best meets your wishes and your spouse's and kids' needs, it's important that everyone knows why you decided to do what you did.

These things are especially important when you're planning to leave retirement account assets behind in a way that assures you'll provide for your spouse and your kids.

◆ If your kids are young, make sure you have enough life insurance that names them or a trust for their benefit as beneficiaries. If you're in moderately good health, term life insurance is cheap. With enough coverage, you can decide to take advantage of the estate and income tax advantages of leaving your retirement accounts to your spouse without ignoring the financial needs of your kids.

◆ If your spouse is younger than you, don't assume that your kids will ever see the money from your retirement accounts on which they're listed as contingent beneficiaries. Your younger spouse may need most or all of your retirement assets for her own support. If you have a specific amount you want to give your kids, keep that amount in a separate account that names them specifically as primary beneficiaries.

◆ Don't sell your spouse short to please your kids. Don't automatically leave all your money to your kids without considering the financial needs of your second spouse. Remember that your spouse could incur medical costs or other expenses. Don't set her up for a financially insecure retirement if hardship strikes after you're gone.

◆ Keep in mind that your spouse can inherit some retirement assets more cheaply than your kids. Your kids may be able to continue the tax benefits of an IRA or a Roth account, but in many cases only a spouse can roll over a work plan like a 401(k) or a 403(b) to her benefit without tax. The same applies to pension benefits.

The Least You Need to Know

◆ The plan document will say whether a beneficiary can stretch retirement plan withdrawals out over her lifetime or whether she must empty the account within five years.

◆ Specifically list plan beneficiaries in the beneficiary designation paperwork.

◆ The plan trustees will confirm beneficiary changes that you make in writing.

◆ Many IRAs and some work plans will let you assign complex beneficiary designations if you ask them.

◆ Life insurance is a good way to be sure your young kids are financially secure if you want to leave your retirement accounts to your second spouse.

Chapter 14

Inherited IRAs

In This Chapter

- ◆ Inheriting an IRA or a work retirement plan
- ◆ Making choices regarding your inheritance with your long-term financial goals in mind
- ◆ Options for spouses, children, and other nonspouse beneficiaries
- ◆ Avoiding costly common mistakes

If you've recently inherited a retirement account, you probably have mixed feelings about your windfall amid the grief of loss. But realize that the person who named you as beneficiary probably thought quite carefully about his choice, so it's just as important for you to think carefully about what to do with the account now that it's been passed to you.

Fortunately, the IRS understands it can take time to decide with a clear mind what you want to do with your money. You only need to attend to a few things in relatively short order; then you have some time to collect the information you need in order to decide what to do with your inheritance.

Step One: Stop and Think

You should always avoid making quick decisions when it comes to your finances, but especially if you inherit a retirement account. If you plan with care, you can continue to take advantage of the tax-benefited growth in the account that the owner started. Penalties for making a mistake with a distribution can be steep. So it's important to watch for four important deadlines: the nine-month anniversary of the account owner's death, December 31 of the year the account owner died, and October 31 and December 31 of the following year. Keep an eye toward these important dates, and be sure to spend time you need gathering all the information about your options and getting good advice before executing your plan.

Immediate Steps

You need to take six basic steps as soon as possible after a retirement account owner dies. This timeline is mainly driven by the need to make sure you have enough time to complete any required distributions before the end of the year, but it also works as a good first step to organizing the person's estate.

1. Collect all the financial information you can find. Pay particular attention to the values of the retirement accounts. Eventually, you'll want a complete list of all accounts, each account's beneficiaries, the value of the accounts when the person died, the value of the account as of the previous December 31, and whether the account has any basis. The basis is the amount you can withdraw from the account without paying taxes. (See Chapter 3 for more detail.) Other information you need to note related to the retirement accounts is the person's age when he died, his date of birth, and, if he has one, the date he opened his Roth IRA account.

2. If the person was past age $70\frac{1}{2}$ when he died, his required minimum distribution or RMD needs to be made for the year he died. His account statement or statements will show whether or not he made a distribution. If a distribution must still be made, the executor will need to contact the financial institution. Be sure that an RMD is made from each retirement account or that one RMD

is made covering the total of all accounts. You don't need to worry about RMD in this case if the account was a Roth (see Chapter 3).

3. The primary beneficiary has nine months after the account holder's death to refuse—or disclaim—the inheritance in order to have the account pass to the contingent beneficiary. If you think this might be a good estate planning option for you, do some financial planning in the short term so you can make a decision and let the executor and the retirement plan trustees know. This option is helpful if the primary beneficiary has her own income and doesn't need the assets from the IRA; it could be a good tax-saving strategy to pass the inheritance to the contingent beneficiaries.

> **Nest Eggs**
>
> If you're the executor, you need an estate lawyer to help you. Contact the lawyer who created the will or check with your state bar association for a list of estate lawyers near you. Find your state bar association easily online with a web search of your state's name and "state bar association."

4. You have until December 31 of the year after the account holder died—for example, if the account holder died December 12, 2008, you have until December 12, 2009, to start taking your own RMDs based on your life expectancy. You need to start taking these withdrawals even if the account holder was under age 70½ when she died. If there was more than one beneficiary of the retirement account, this is also the deadline for each to set up their own inherited IRA so that RMDs can be calculated on their own life expectancy. If you miss this deadline, you can still set up separate accounts, but the RMD calculation must then be figured on the oldest beneficiary's life expectancy. Depending on circumstances, this might make your RMD (and the taxes due on the RMD) bigger. Be very careful about how you title your new inherited IRA account (the account trustee will help you). If you title your inherited IRA wrong, you won't get the chance to stretch your RMDs over your lifetime. More on this next.

5. If a trust is the beneficiary of the account instead of a person, October 31 the year after the account holder died is the deadline for submitting the trust information to the account trustee. The account trustee has to determine whether or not the trust qualifies for favorable RMD treatment.

6. Start collecting the advisors you'll use to help you make choices about your inheritance. Contact your financial planner, your accountant, and the executor of the estate.

Assess Your Options

Once you've organized the basic information about the retirement accounts you're inheriting, find out what options are available to you as beneficiary. These options could include:

◆ Withdrawing the balance, making a lump sum distribution of the account right away.

◆ Taking distributions over five years.

◆ Taking distributions over your lifetime or at the same pace that the original account owner had already begun taking them.

The retirement plan trustee can answer these questions by referencing the plan document or the employer if the account is a work plan like a 401(k), 403(b), or 457 plan. Once you notify the trustee that the account owner has died, he will usually send a packet of information to the beneficiary (you) with the options you can choose for the account and a list of the documents you'll need to complete the distribution. These documents are often just simply the death certificate and information on where the money is to be transferred.

Rainy Days

Sixty-day rollovers are not available with retirement account money that you inherit. Only direct trustee-to-trustee transfers can be made without triggering tax on the distribution. If the trustee insists on cutting a check instead of making an electronic transfer, be sure he makes the check out to your retirement account and not to you personally, for example, "Fidelity Investments for the benefit of John Smith."

Except in the case of the lump sum distribution, you'll need a new account to receive the money. The trustee will include an account application to encourage you to keep the money with his institution, but you're not required to. You can choose your own retirement account trustee (see Chapter 3).

Once you know your distribution options, you need to figure out the tax ramifications of your choices before deciding which will work best for you. You're taxed on withdrawals from the retirement accounts in the same way the original owner would have been, except you won't owe the extra 10 percent penalty for being under age 59½. And just like making an IRA direct trustee-to-trustee transfer out of your own account, as long as you keep the money in a retirement plan, you keep the tax deferral.

There are three key tax-related things to keep in mind when deciding when and how to manage your inherited retirement account:

- You pay income taxes on the amount of money that you distribute from the retirement account (and don't transfer to another IRA).

- You don't pay taxes on the principal of a Roth account, and only pay income taxes on any earnings you distribute if the account isn't at least five years old.

- If the retirement account has a basis—the amount that was deposited after-tax—you can withdraw that amount tax-free on a pro-rata basis of all your IRA balances. Check the account owner's tax return for form 8606 to see if there is a basis in the account.

Unless you need the money right away, your goal should be to save taxes by continuing the tax deferral in your own retirement account or what's called a "beneficiary" or "inherited" IRA for as long as you can.

Planning for the Long Term

You have time to do some planning before deciding what to do with your retirement plan inheritance. If you're required to start taking distributions, make sure you take a minimum distribution before the end of the year following the year the original account holder died.

This will preserve your chance to take distributions over your lifetime or according to the account holder's original life expectancy, as specified in charts created by the IRS and available through its website, www.IRS.gov. If you forget or for some other reason don't take the distribution, you'll be required to empty the account by the fifth year, potentially giving up a lot of tax benefit.

If you're the widowed spouse, you can transfer the retirement money inheritance into your own account and continue as if it were originally yours, deferring withdrawals or taking the RMD if you're over age 70½. If you're not the spouse, take some time to figure out how to best stretch the tax benefits of the IRA even if you can't keep the money completely within a retirement fund and must make withdrawals.

If the custodian or the tax law requires you to give up some tax benefit by taking the money out over time, but you're still working and are not already maxing out your retirement contributions, add more to the retirement accounts you're eligible for to get the tax benefit. In this case, the living expenses you would have paid with your salary could be covered by your inheritance, and your wages could fund your retirement account.

If the retirement plan you're inheriting was invested in an annuity instead of something more liquid like a mutual fund or a certificate of deposit, the insurance company trustee will offer you withdrawal options based on the annuity product itself. Carefully compare the convenience of having the insurance company manage the withdrawals with the high cost of staying with them. Also compare the effort of managing the withdrawals yourself to the cost of paying a financial planner or investment advisor to help you.

What Spouses and Nonspouses Need to Know

A spouse who is inheriting IRAs has the advantage of being able to transfer retirement accounts she's inherited without owing estate taxes or any more income tax than her late spouse would have owed on the account. This doesn't mean that she should take advantage of this rule without careful planning. Disclaiming the inheritance so that the accounts can pass to contingent beneficiaries like the children could be a better option in the long term.

A nonspouse beneficiary needs to carefully consider her own financial plan and the tax ramifications of bringing her inheritance into her own retirement nest egg.

Whether you have a carefully thought-out estate and retirement plan or this is your first look at the finances, consider these important points when you inherit a retirement account. The approach you take differs whether you're the widowed spouse, one of the kids, a relative, or a friend.

Rules for Spouses

If you've recently lost your spouse, sitting down to do a full financial plan, much less thinking about long-term life and financial goals, may seem overwhelming. Fortunately, the review of your plan doesn't need to be as detailed and involved as future reviews will be when you're ready to tackle them. Follow these short-term steps to decide whether it would be better to transfer the accounts to your name or disclaim and let the assets go to the contingent beneficiaries.

- ◆ **Do you need the money?** This may seem like a simple question, but many widows and widowers ignore it. Don't be too quick to pass inheritances to the next generation if you need the money for your own retirement security. If you're still working or you're many years from retirement, run one of the retirement calculators on www.CalcXML.com or www.AARP.com to get an idea of whether you're on track for retirement or still have a good deal of catching up to do. Keep the retirement inheritance if it looks like you don't have enough set aside for your own secure retirement or that you might just barely make it. If you're lucky enough to have much more than you think you'll need, plan a meeting with your financial planner to double-check your numbers, and then consider disclaiming your inheritance.

  If you're retired, check your monthly expenses and income sources. Gather your credit card statements, bank statements, and checkbooks, and make an estimate of what is coming in and what has been going out. If you want to be more detailed, an account aggregator like www.Mint.com can help you with this by categorizing your expenses into an easy-to-read pie chart. If your nest egg is smaller than 25 times the annual income you need from investments, keep your inheritance and transfer the accounts to your name.

♦ Do you expect to receive other inheritances? Families need to talk about money, but few do. If you think you might also inherit money from another source, like your own parents or in-laws, do some planning with them before deciding whether to take or disclaim the inheritance from your spouse. You may never have considered ever talking so openly with family about money, but it would be a shame to act on an assumption of a sizable inheritance that turns out to be false and have it cost the family money or estate taxes.

Once the IRA is updated to show you as the inherited owner of the IRA, you can name your own beneficiaries. This is the time to complete a fully updated financial plan, with the help of a financial planner if necessary, to decide what your asset allocation should be and, if you're retired, what your withdrawals should be, and to update your estate plan. When you've done that, you may decide to name primary beneficiaries of your kids, other important people, a charity, or a trust.

Nest Eggs

If you're inheriting a Roth IRA and you're under age 59½, you're eligible to take money from the Roth tax-free as long as the account has met the five-year rule.

Tips for the Kids

If you're not the spouse, the options of what you can do with your retirement plan inheritance will all involve some tax planning. You may have the option of taking small distributions over your lifetime, or you may have to take the balance out of the account within five years. Since you'll owe income tax on the money you withdraw from the IRA (not including any basis in the IRA as mentioned previously), it's best to try to limit the amount you take out of the account. Keeping the IRA intact will save taxes and can help grow a nest egg for your own retirement. Most trustees will give you the option of taking RMD over your lifetime starting in the year after the year the original owner died, or to take a full distribution within five years. The lifetime option is usually the best choice because it keeps the money in the IRA longer. Avoid taking any more money than you have to in order to preserve as much of the tax benefits of the account as you can.

If you're inheriting the retirement account alone or with others—particularly if the beneficiaries vary in age by more than a few years—you need to ask the trustee to open an inherited IRA for each individual by December 31 of the year after the original account owner died. Be very careful how the new inherited IRA is titled. The original owner's name stays on the account, but the name of the beneficiary is added. For example, the "John Smith, deceased, IRA, for the benefit of Daughter Smith, beneficiary." The wording may be different depending on your trustee, but it should be clear that it is not Daughter's IRA in this case, but an inherited IRA. The transfer into the inherited IRA should be a trustee-to-trustee transfer; the trustee can't send you a check. If they do send a check made out to you in your name, then the IRS deems that as a distribution—you can't put it back into the account, and you can't put it in your own IRA. Some trustees will send a check made out to the inherited IRA. You can redeposit the check in the properly titled inherited IRA in that case, but the trustee-to-trustee transfer is preferred to avoid confusion.

Estate executors often delay distributing assets to the beneficiaries until they have the estate nearly settled and know they have enough money to cover any estate taxes or other obligations. Be ready for the executor to come back to you and your inherited IRA if they need to for taxes. Other than making the RMD, don't withdraw the money too quickly; the executor may need some money to pay estate taxes.

The tax law offers a credit to beneficiaries who are forced to withdraw money from IRAs they've inherited to pay estate taxes. The law recognizes that the beneficiaries are, in a sense, being double-taxed—first when they pay income tax on the amount they withdraw from the IRA and again when they pay the estate tax. Dividing the IRA assets so each beneficiary has a separate account makes the bookkeeping on this credit easier. If estate taxes are due and the retirement accounts are the only assets available to pay them, then having separate accounts will make it easier for each beneficiary to apply the potential tax credit on his personal tax return.

Guard Against the Common Mistakes

Beyond being sure you follow the sticky tax laws that govern retirement plan inheritances, you need to avoid making these six big mistakes when you inherit a retirement account.

◆ **Taking more than absolutely necessary out of the accounts.** Unless you're the spouse and the retirement assets are part of your family financial plan, most inheritances are essentially found money. It will help your finances much more in the long term if you carefully plan to keep the accounts or their value growing rather than spending an inheritance. Increase your investments in other accounts with the money you must withdraw from your beneficiary IRA. Increase your contributions to your work plan; if you're retired, decrease your withdrawals from other investments. If you're already maxing your work plan without factoring in the cash flow generated by the inheritance, invest in a Roth IRA or a nondeductible IRA or make deposits to your taxable investment account.

◆ **Giving money away without careful planning.** Try to avoid making any large or irrevocable decisions within the first two to three years after losing your spouse. Giving money away to your kids, family, or a charity may seem like the best way to honor your late spouse, but all those things can wait until you have had time to clearly review your own new financial goals and financial situation. Don't rush.

◆ **Not having taxes withheld from retirement account withdrawals.** The trustee will offer to withhold income taxes from the distributions you take in cash from the retirement account. Take them up on the offer. This withholding could save you from having to make separate estimated tax payments on the withdrawals or, worse yet, being surprised by the taxes you owe when you file your tax return. The standard percentage they withhold may still not be enough, though. Check last year's tax return to see what bracket you're in without the distribution income. Then add the withdrawals you're taking to your total taxable income (page two of the tax return), and check the marginal tax bracket chart to see the rate that the new withdrawals will really be taxed at. The trustee can withhold more than the standard amount if you ask him to.

◆ Holding the investments of the inherited account. Many beneficiaries don't know that it's okay to change the investments in
  the account you're inheriting. Your goals and time frame are
  probably different than the goals and time frame of the original
  account owner. Even if you're the widowed spouse, your new circumstances could dictate a change in investment strategy. Don't
  keep inappropriate investments in the account just because your
  loved one bought them and they have always done well. There's a
  chance he may have wanted to sell some of the investments. And
  even if he hadn't, he probably would prefer you get the financial
  security he intended to give you from the account.

◆ Retaining the same investment manager. Once you've inherited an
  IRA, remember that you don't have to stay with the same investment manager and you don't have to manage the account yourself.
  Decide how you want to manage the account based on what you
  want to do and what makes you feel comfortable. If your loved
  one got financial advice from an investment advisor or financial
  planner you like, you might want to continue using that person or
  company. If not, find an advisor you like. Chances are, your loved
  one was only concerned that you have the security the inheritance
  would provide and was less concerned about how you managed the
  account as long as you manage it for your greatest benefit.

◆ Falling for ploys. Some beneficiaries, particularly spouses who
  have not been closely involved with the family finances, are sus-
  ceptible to sketchy investment schemes that promise to save you
  money. Economists expect a huge amount of wealth to be passed
  between generations over the next 30 years, and the wolves have
  already started circling. Don't invest in anything you don't understand or that promises returns or tax savings that are dramatically
  greater than what other investments are offering. If you're distraught about losing your loved one, you're not in the right frame
  of mind to focus on and research a new investment. Check on
  the short-term tax tasks that you need to attend to—like getting
  the RMD made, if it has to be—and then give yourself time to
  adjust before diving into managing your accounts and buying new
  investments.

The Least You Need to Know

♦ The plan trustee—the investment firm, or the employer—is the best resource for finding out what your options are in receiving your inheritance from a retirement account.

♦ If the original account holder was taking required minimum distributions (RMDs) or was past age $70\frac{1}{2}$, you need to make a distribution for the year he died before December 31.

♦ Other than checking that the RMD has been made, money doesn't need to be distributed from a retirement account until December 31 of the year following the account owner's death.

♦ Most beneficiaries will have the option of continuing the great tax-deferred benefits of the retirement account they inherit by transferring it into their own IRA as a spouse or into a beneficiary IRA, also called an inherited IRA, as a nonspouse.

♦ If the only primary beneficiary is the spouse, then the account can be transferred to her without income or estate tax being due.

Appendix A

Glossary

401(a) plan A retirement account with many of the characteristics of a 403(b) plan, except that only the employer may contribute to the 401(a).

401(k) plans Broad label for a variety of employer-sponsored retirement savings incentive programs.

403(b) plan A retirement plan available to employees of public schools, nonprofit organizations, or the clergy. It is identical to the 401(k), except that employers need not contribute, and they aren't subject to 401(k)'s stringent Employee Retirement Income Security Act (ERISA) rules.

457 deferred-compensation plan Sometimes called a deferred-comp plan, this retirement plan defers an employee's pay by the amount contributed, a characteristic shared by 401(k) and SIMPLE plans.

457(b) plan This variation of a 457 deferred-compensation plan is provided by state and local governments.

457(f) plan A variation of a 457 deferred-compensation plan offered by large, tax-exempt organizations like hospitals and universities, usually for their upper management employees. They also are most often used to attract and retain high-level executives.

72(t)   An IRA-related strategy that enables avoidance of the 10 percent penalty on withdrawals as long as account holders make a series of substantially equal withdrawals at least annually.

account aggregator   An online platform that presents data from multiple accounts in a single interface that stores log-in information and simplifies web access to personal financial information.

active management   An investment management style that presumes that investments guided by a fund manager and informed by industry and economic insight should perform better than other similar investments.

adjusted gross income (AGI)   The amount of income calculated by adding work income and other income such as investment interest and dividends or alimony. It excludes such things as alimony paid and the cost of health insurance paid by the self-employed.

administrative fee   This fee covers the cost of running the plan itself, including expenses such as the cost of preparing annual reports, running required discrimination tests, and supporting the website and customer service department.

after-tax contribution   A contribution to an IRA that is not deductible from a filer's tax obligation.

alternative minimum tax   A tax created to close loopholes that enabled some super-rich taxpayers to pay unfairly low or even no taxes by resorting to legal tax shelters. Unfortunately, the tax lacks indexes to inflation, making more middle-class families vulnerable to assessment.

annual expense ratio   The percentage of plan assets that are paid to cover operating, management, and marketing costs.

asset allocation   An investment recipe for all an individual's accounts, dictating the percentage of a portfolio invested in stocks, bonds, or cash.

benchmark   A standard used to compare performance, such as the Standard and Poor's 500 Index.

capital gain tax rate   The percentage of investing profits that must be paid in taxes, calculated as a proportion of the profit or capital gain of an investment.

certificate of deposit   A bank's promissory note to repay the amount deposited, with interest, at a future date, typically one month to five years away.

cliff vesting   A vesting schedule in which none of an employer's contribution becomes an asset of the employee until the employee reaches a specified work anniversary. At the anniversary date, the employer's full contribution belongs to the employee.

compound interest   An investment principal in which interest is paid not only on the principal saved but also on the accumulated interest from prior periods that has not been withdrawn.

contribution   The amount of cash or other assets deposited in a retirement account.

defined-benefit plan   A retirement plan such as a traditional pension that pays a specific retirement benefit once certain requirements such as years of service or age are met.

defined-contribution plan   A retirement plan incorporating specific rules that dictate when deposits can be made, who can make them, and how big the deposit can be.

direct-transfer rollover   Also known as a trustee-to-trustee transfer, a process that directly moves assets from a 401(k) plan to an individual retirement account.

dollar-cost averaging   A savings strategy involving investing the same dollar amount at fixed intervals. As share prices fluctuate, dollar-cost averaging boosts investment performance by buying fewer shares when prices are up and more shares when prices are down.

Employee Retirement Income Security Act (ERISA)   This federal law sets the standards for employee retirement and health-care benefits.

exchange-traded funds (ETFs)   Pooled investment accounts that resemble mutual funds in that they hold a basket of many individual investments but that are traded directly on the stock exchanges by investors buying and selling their shares like stocks.

fee-only financial planner   A financial advisor who charges only for his advice, based on the consultation duration or project scope, and who doesn't sell investment products for commission in order to avoid conflict of interest in investment choice recommendations.

fixed annuity   A tax-deferred financial instrument marketed by insurance companies that pays a fixed rate of interest and that readjusts on a yearly basis.

graded vesting   A vesting schedule in which an employer's contribution vests gradually over time, in stages or grades.

income tax rate   The percentage of one's income that must be paid to local, state, or federal government.

individual retirement accounts (IRA)   Retirement plan accounts that carry a tax advantage intended to encourage savings.

IRA basis   The amount contributed to an IRA that isn't eligible for tax deduction.

IRA trustee fees   Costs paid by the investor that can include sales commissions, management fees, and a "12-b1" marketing fee.

lifestyle funds   Investment pools that resemble target-date funds in that they are a mix of mutual funds in an asset allocation that the mutual fund company chooses but that cater to risk tolerances.

marginal tax rate   The rate on the highest bracket a taxpayer's income reached.

matching contribution   An employer plan-match option under which an employer promises to match a certain percentage of each employee's contribution up to a specific percentage of their pay.

medical IRA   Also known as a health savings account, an individual retirement account in which account holders can deposit pretax money to pay for medical expenses.

modified adjusted gross income   Also known as modified AGI, the adjusted gross income from an IRA withdrawal by someone age 59½ or older, disabled or deceased, using the withdrawals to pay for college or other qualified higher education expenses, or using withdrawals toward a first-time home purchase.

money market deposit account   An investment account that often pays lower interest than a CD, but whose assets are accessible anytime without waiting for a future maturity date.

Monte Carlo calculator   A calculator that generates a measure of the probability that a given investment outcome scenario will result in a financially comfortable retirement based on expected assets, probable lifetime, and economic conditions.

monthly money meeting (M&Ms)   A monthly financial review during which individuals, spouses, partners, and perhaps children review and update financial and retirement goals. Meetings should review income and expenses, discuss upcoming expenses and long-term spending goals, and assess cash allowances

mutual funds   A combination of individual investments—stocks, bonds, and cash—bundled together into one product.

nonretirement accounts   Bank or mutual fund accounts that are not held inside IRAs and on which taxes must be paid as accrued.

passive management   An investment management style that presumes that fund managers are unlikely to consistently outperform the market over the long term and that seeks to simply match the market's performance.

plan provider   The company hired to administer an employer-sponsored retirement plan, often acting as the plan trustee and handling the back-office operations required of a 401(k) plan.

pretax contribution   A contribution to an IRA that a filer is permitted to deduct from his tax obligation.

prime rate   The interest rate commercial banks charge their best customers, generally large companies.

profit-sharing contribution   An employer plan-match option that enables employers to decide each year whether to contribute to the employees' plans.

QUADRO   Formally known as a qualified domestic relation order, a divorce-specific transfer between two people's accounts requiring a court order.

rebalancing   Adjustments to an asset allocation that correct for different assets having performed differently over time, eventually comprising different portfolio percentages than intended.

Roth 401(k)   An employer-sponsored retirement account in which tax liability accrues upon contribution but whose account earnings and withdrawals are tax-free.

Roth 403(b)   An employer-sponsored retirement account offered to employees of public schools, nonprofit organizations, and the clergy in which tax liability accrues upon contribution but whose account earnings and withdrawals are tax-free.

Roth IRA   A form of individual retirement account in which taxes do not accrue on withdrawn funds, whether earnings or basis.

safe-harbor 401(k)   An employee-sponsored plan that reduces an employer's effort and cost in running the plan's nondiscrimination tests.

SEP plan   Formally known as the Simplified Employee Pension plan, a retirement option popular with people who are self-employed and who don't have employees in which 100 percent of the contributions come from the employer.

SIMPLE 401(k) plan   A retirement plan that combines the features of SIMPLE IRAs and regular 401(k) plans, including contribution limits and employer match rules of SIMPLE plans.

SIMPLE plan   Formally known as the Savings Incentive Match Plan for Employees, a common option in companies with 30 or fewer employees but available to companies with up to 100 employees, an IRA account into which both employee and employer can contribute.

single-person 401(k)   Also called a solo 401(k) and a self-employed 401(k), a retirement plan that simplifies the administration of a 401(k) enough to make it affordable for single-person companies and very small enterprises.

60-day rollover   A transfer of assets from a 401(k) plan to an individual retirement account that permits use of the money during a 60-day period and that assesses a 10 percent early withdrawal penalty unless the rollover is completed before the 60-day period ends.

Summary Plan Description (SPD)   The book of rules that governs your specific 401(k) plan, including when an employee will be eligible to participate and the specifics about how to contribute to the account and how money can be withdrawn.

target-date fund   A mutual fund whose allocations of stocks, bonds, and cash are tailored to perform best with a time-specific event, such as retirement, in mind.

tax-deductible   The quality of income or capital gains generated by investments that can reduce tax liability by the amount deposited into a retirement account.

tax-deferred   The quality of income or capital gains generated by investments that do not become taxable under law until funds are withdrawn from an account.

taxable income   The earnings from an individual's job and from interest or dividends from his investments on which he must pay tax each year.

variable annuities   A tax-deferred financial instrument marketed by insurance companies that contains a basket of individual stock or bond investments called sub-accounts and that change in value based on the performance of the investments in the sub-accounts.

withdrawal   The cash value of an asset redeemed from a retirement account.

Web Resources

We've listed some of our favorite resources here. Remember, sometimes a little information can be a dangerous thing, and making a mistake with your money can be costly. Be sure to cross-check several resources to confirm the information you find and your interpretation of it. When in doubt, check with your financial advisor, accountant, or lawyer.

Calculators and Asset Allocation Tools

These sites have a calculator for practically every need. Here, you can calculate your retirement nest egg, decide on an asset allocation, target your college savings plan, and more.

Choose to Save—www.choosetosave.org/calculators/

KJE Computer Solutions Financial Calculators—www. dinkytown.net

Financial Calculators—www.fincalc.com

Account Aggregators

Account aggregators make organizing your accounts and tracking your expenses easy, no matter how many accounts you have. The aggregator will show all of your linked accounts on one web page and will automatically assign categories to the transactions in each account. Aggregators are an easy way to check your spending, especially if you have several bank and credit card accounts to keep track of.

Yodlee Money Center—www.yodlee.com

Mint Software, Inc.—www.mint.com

Asset Allocation and Investing

U.S. Securities and Exchange Commission—www.sec.gov

Asset Allocation at SEC.gov—www.sec.gov/investor/pubs.shtml

Securities Regulations Advice—www.sec-nasd-regulations.com

Financial Industry Regulatory Authority—www.finra.org

The Motley Fool—www.fool.com/investing.htm

Treasury Direct—www.treasurydirect.gov

Morningstar: Stocks, mutual funds and investing—www.morningstar.com

American Stock Exchange—www.amex.com

Retirement Planning

We like these websites for retirement planning education. Some of them include calculators to help estimate how much money you need to retire.

Analyze Now—www.analyzenow.com

About.com Retirement planning—www.retireplan.about.com

AARP's Financial Planning—www.aarp.org/financial

U.S. Social Security Administration—www.ssa.gov

Bankrate.com—www.bankrate.com/retirement

The Vanguard Group—www.personal.vanguard.com/retirement

Fidelity Investments—www.personal.fidelity.com/retirement

Wiser Women—www.wiserwomen.com

Flexible Retirement Planner—www.flexibleRetirementPlanner.com

National Center for Policy Analysis—www.retirementreform.org

Hiring Professional Advice

Here are some sites that will help you find an advisor to help you. Each association provides referrals to its members in your area. Check the sites for a list of questions to ask your potential advisor and for information on their credentials.

National Association of Personal Financial Advisors—www.napfa.org

The Financial Planning Association—www.fpanet.org

American Institute of Certified Public Accountants—www.aicpa.org

The National Association of Enrolled Agents—www.naea.org

The American Bar Association—www.abanet.org

Find Law Lawyer Directory—www.lawyers.findlaw.com

Independent Insurance Agents & Brokers of America—www.iiaba.net

National Association of Professional Organizers—www.napo.net

The American Institute of Professional Bookkeepers—www.aipb.org

National Elder Law Foundation—www.nelf.org

Financial Sites, Newsletters, and Blogs

The more you read about your money, the more you'll learn and the better off you'll be. Remember, not everything in print is true and it won't always apply to your situation.

Smart Money—www.smartmoney.com

MarketWatch—www.marketwatch.com

Wall Street Journal—www.wsj.com

MSN Money—www.moneycentral.msn.com

Women's Financial Network—www.wfn.com/index.asp

Jim Lowell's Fidelity Investor—www.fidelityinvestor.com

The Independent Advisor for Vanguard Investors—www.adviseronline. com

WIFE E-Newsletter, "A Man Is Not a Financial Plan"—www.wife.org/ subscribe.htm

Jennifer's Compass Blog by Jennifer Lane CFP—www.jenniferscompass. typepad.com

Online Money Market Accounts

These online banks may offer higher interest than your local bank for your long-term savings.

ING Direct—www.ingdirect.com

Emigrant Bank—www.emigrantdirect.com

HSBC Bank—www.hsbc.com

Bankrate—www.bankrate.com

Real Estate

Check out these sites for an estimate of what your home is worth, what is on sale in your area, or to check prices in the area you'd like to retire to. You can also check here to learn more about ways to access the equity in your home in retirement and the dangers of reverse mortgages.

Zillow—www.zillow.com

AARP Reverse Mortgage—www.aarp.org/money/revmort

U.S. Department of Housing and Urban Development—www.hud.gov

National Association of Realtors—www.realtor.org

Taxes and Information on Retirement Plans

The IRA and the Department of Labor are the final word on the laws regulating your retirement plan, but these other sites might make interpreting what you find at IRS.gov and Dol.gov easier to understand.

Internal Revenue Service—www.irs.gov

Department of Labor—www.dol.gov

Tax Guide for Investors—www.fairmark.com/amt

Accountants World—www.accountantsworld.com

World Wide Web Tax—www.wwwebtax.com

Don't Mess with Taxes—www.dontmesswithtaxes.typepad.com

Inherited IRA Info—www.inherited-ira.info

Retirement Plan Blog—www.retirementplanblog.com

Rollover IRA—www.rollover-ira.info

Health Savings Accounts—www.health-savings-accounts.com

Estate Planning and Elder Law

Elder law and estate law are two very important areas of law that have a big impact on your retirement security. These sites will help you understand the issues affecting you and will help you find a lawyer to advise you.

Elder Law Attorney with the National Elder Law Foundation—www.nelf.org

ElderLawAnswers—www.elderlawanswers.com

Nolo's Everyday Estate Planning Blog—www.blogs.nolo.com/estateplanning

Elder Law Answers blog—www.hmargolis.typepad.com/elderlawanswers_blog/

Online Education

These sites are specifically geared to education. They're great resources to help you learn more.

U.S. Financial Literacy and Education Commission—www.mymoney.gov

National Endowment for Financial Education—www.nefe.org

Federal Reserve Education—www.federalreserveeducation.org

Institute of Consumer Financial Education—www.financial-education-icfe.org

National Association of Investors—www.better-investing.org

Investment Clubs and the SEC—www.sec.gov/investor/pubs/invclub.htm

Divorce

Divorce is seldom cheap and is never easy. Learn more about how divorce can affect your retirement accounts at these sites.

Divorce Net: Family Law Information—www.divorcenet.com

Nolo's Divorce, Custody, and Family Law Blog—www.blogs.nolo.com/divorcefamily

Widowhood

Losing a spouse, a partner, or a family member can leave you feeling overwhelmed with the financial decisions you have to make. These sites have information about Social Security benefits and other things you need to know when you lose a loved one.

Social Security Survivors Benefit Info—www.ssa.gov

Widow Net—www.widownet.org

AARP's Family, Home, and Legal—www.aarp.org/families

When a Loved One Dies Checklist—www.printablechecklists.com/checklist87.shtml

Staying the Course When the Economy Gets Choppy

Despite the historical upward trend in the price of stocks, it's clear the stock market makes no guarantee of investment growth from month to month or even year to year. The stock market and the economy go through waves of growth and decline on a surprisingly regular pattern—so regular, in fact, that this ebb and flow is known as an "economic cycle." It's comparatively easy to invest successfully on the growth curve of the cycle, when the stock market is growing in value and your savings are increasing. But investors, even professional ones, can get spooked when stock prices drop—especially if they drop faster and for longer periods than most investors have personally seen before—and the economy moves into the decline curve of its cycle. A big part of your financial success will turn on whether you can stick to your plan even when the stock market and the economy seem to be coming unhinged.

There are five fundamental steps you should take if you feel like a decline in the stock market or an economic recession is tempting you to abandon your investment plan and sell your stock investments. They're basic principles that mirror concepts we deal with in depth elsewhere in this book, but they bear repeating in a discussion about how to gear your expectations and emotional responses to an economic slump.

1. Understand your account statements

2. Don't change your plan contributions

3. Turn off the "auto-rebalance" feature

4. Don't buy anything you don't need

5. Track expenses

Understand Your Account Statements

In painful stock market slumps, individual investors' first instinct is often to refuse to open their retirement account statements, thinking that the sight of a declining account balance will be too painful. You must remember that month-to-month fluctuations in your investment account balance are normal if your investments include stocks. That's the nature of stocks themselves: over short periods like a month, a quarter, or even a year, they can lose value. The reason you have stocks as part of your asset allocation is for their growth over the long term and their ability to hedge against long-term inflation. The role of stocks in your portfolio is not to earn you predictable interest or dividends in a particular month.

Keep that in mind when you read your monthly or quarterly account statements. The part of the portfolio that you've designated for investments in stocks is for the long term; the part that is allocated to bonds and cash is for use in the nearer future. For example, if you're getting ready to retire soon, you're looking to the bonds and cash in your account for income at the start of retirement and then you'll sell the stocks in later years. The stocks are part of your portfolio, so they will unquestionably affect the bottom line of your account statement; but if you've planned your asset allocation carefully, a temporary drop in stock prices shouldn't affect your financial security.

When you look at your account statements, focus less on the bottom line than the percentage change in the balance. Ask yourself, "Is my portfolio going down as I would expect based on how the market indexes have fared?" For example, if the stock market is down 25 percent for the year and your portfolio holds 60 percent stock, does your stock allocation roughly mirror the overall market's decline? Look solely at the stock investments in your portfolio. If those investments have declined more dramatically than the most similar stock market index—the Dow Jones Industrial Average, for example, or the S&P 500—it is important that you review the quality of your mutual funds or other portfolio investments. If they have declined roughly the same amount as the market, then you probably don't need to make a change.

Don't Change Your Plan Contributions

Dollar-cost averaging—making regular investments of the same amount on a regular cycle—is an important part of a successful investment plan. If you're investing a consistent amount, as the market goes down, your investments will buy more shares of now-cheaper stocks. When the market rises, you'll buy fewer of the more expensive shares. Over time, your average cost per share will be lower under this strategy, helping to boost your overall returns. This is a powerful strategy but can be a difficult one to follow when the market is dropping and your balance is staying the same or dropping with it, despite your new deposits. It can feel like you're making your contributions into a black hole. The temptation can be to stop adding to your account until the market recovers. The flaw in that reasoning is, if you stop investing in the declining market only to resume in the rising market, you'll miss out on the cheaper shares. In essence, you'll be missing out on the "bargain basement" sale on stocks that the market is holding as it tries to win back customers.

What's more, once you stop investing, you're likely to wait too long to start again. For many people, once they stop an investment plan, the money they were investing gets reabsorbed into their monthly spending. If this happens to you, you might find that when you decide the time is right to restart your contributions, you can no longer afford to because the money you once earmarked for investments has begun to pay for part of your lifestyle—a real problem.

For all these reasons, the best course through a downturn in the market is to stay with your contributions. But if the bottom line for you is that your account balance declines are keeping you awake at night and you just have to do something, there are two options you might consider: adjust your plan so your future contributions go to a more conservative investment, or split your contributions between the investment account and your savings or an account to pay down debt.

In the first option, changing your investment so that new contributions are invested more conservatively won't help you take full advantage of dollar-cost averaging, but it will help your account feel less like a black hole, and keeping the regular investments going will keep you in the habit.

The second option will have a similar effect and might work well with your retirement plan at work. If your employer matches your contributions, reduce your new deposits to the minimum amount they will match, and then set up a direct deposit from your paycheck for the remaining amount you were investing and put it toward building savings or paying down debt. This way you won't miss out on the automatic return of getting the employer match, you'll stay in the habit of saving and investing the same amount of money, and you'll build your emergency fund or pay down debt—always a good thing in times when the stock market is down.

Turn Off the "Auto-Rebalance" Feature

One of the great features of many work-sponsored retirement plans like 401(k)s and 403(b)s is their "auto-rebalance" feature. This option causes the account to rebalance on a regular basis back to the original target asset allocation you set. Many people choose an annual auto-rebalance schedule so their accounts adjust once per year. If, when the time comes, stocks have fallen in value so that the percentage of stocks in the account is lower than the target, the auto-rebalance will sell some of the bond or cash funds in the account and buy more stock funds to bring everything back into balance.

You don't necessarily have to turn off your auto-rebalance if it's scheduled to reset during a downturn in the market—in fact, it can be an advantage to be buying stocks when they're cheaper and selling bonds when they're high, a fundamental goal of asset allocation. But if you're feeling concerned about a sharp downturn in the market, it can be unnerving to have your account rebalance in the middle of it. Use your judgment and check your emotional comfort level. Remember, an investment plan only works if it's something you can stick with. If rebalancing in the middle of a period of market volatility is going to tempt you to abandon your plan, then turn off the auto-rebalance feature on your account. If you feel you can stay the course, then leave it on and be glad you have the opportunity to buy when stock prices are at bargain levels.

Don't Buy Anything You Don't Need

If the stock market is going down because of an economic recession, then it's important to build up your cash reserves. Recessions are usually fairly brief, so it should only be a short time until the market recovers and the economy starts feeling stronger. In the meantime, reduce your spending on big-ticket items you can wait to buy. Finding less expensive vacation options, toning down gift giving and holiday expenses, shopping for sales on clothing, and using coupons at the grocery store are all good ways to reduce the extras so you can increase savings. It may sound simple, but don't forget to put aside the money you save. Make a point of adding your savings to a money market or savings account instead of just leaving it in your checking account, where it will pose a spending temptation. Seeing the balance build in a separate account as you save will encourage you to save more.

Nest Eggs

Making choices about what to buy now and what expenses to postpone will give you a greater feeling of control over your retirement accounts—something that can be a real help through tough economic times.

Track Your Expenses

Many people don't keep close track of where their money goes. When income is covering expenses without a lot of effort, it's tempting to avoid the hassle of checking on what those expenses actually are. But in an economic downturn, building cash is easier if you know what you're spending on. People are often surprised by how much they spend on things they don't really value. Setting up a simple tracking system using an online account aggregator like Mint.com or Yodlee.com will quickly and easily show you how your money gets spent. Then armed with that information, you can make decisions about what to buy and when to save.

What If Your Partner Disagrees?

Going through an economic rough patch can be unnerving enough without the added stress of disagreements with your partner about what to do next. If you find yourself in disagreement with your partner about how to manage your accounts, start by reviewing, together, your long-term goals. Since investing is for the long term—remember, you shouldn't need the money you've invested in stocks for at least five years—reviewing the long-term goals and how you chose the investment plan to reach them is a good way to try to get both of you back on the same track. Disagreements can emerge if both partners weren't active creators of the plan or if both don't understand the investments used to implement it. Reviewing the plan or the investment analysis together can help bring the less-active partner up to speed and will help make him or her more comfortable with the investment volatility.

A mediator (like the investment advisor who helped you implement the plan), an independent investment advisor or financial planner, or even a new investment advisor (if you created the initial plan on your own) can be helpful if you're finding it difficult as a couple to agree on next steps. The advisor can act as a disinterested third party—not affected by the jitters the tough market might be causing you or your partner to feel—who can review your investments with you and how they fit into your plan. Even if you've always done your own investing, you might find the advisor is a good addition to your team who can help the less investment-savvy partner better understand your investment plan.

If one partner has a dramatically lower risk tolerance, it might help your joint peace of mind to have the more conservative, less volatile investments—like bonds and cash—allocated to his or her accounts while the more volatile stock investments sit in the more risk-tolerant partner's account. So long as you keep the allocation between all your accounts at the target set by your investment plan, having the conservative partner's account in less volatile investments might help him or her feel more certain about sticking to a long-term plan, even when the short term seems less certain.

Market turmoil tends to create a sense of urgency and an impulse to make defensive changes to retirement accounts and long-term investment strategies, almost all of which lead to pitfalls. The five options we've outlined here are proven to help investors stay the course toward retirement security while waiting out the market's rebound. And the ultimate comfort investors should reassure themselves with is that the stock market will inevitably rebound and continue its historical growth trend. Lulls are temporary, but a strong retirement plan, carefully tended, will assure lifelong financial security.

Index

Q-R